The Language of Emily Dickinson

Edited by

Nicole Panizza
Coventry University

and

Trisha Kannan
Independent Scholar

Series in Literary Studies

Copyright © 2021 by the authors.

All rights reserved. No part of this publication may be reproduced, stored in a retrieval system, or transmitted in any form or by any means, electronic, mechanical, photocopying, recording, or otherwise, without the prior permission of Vernon Art and Science Inc.

www.vernonpress.com

In the Americas:
Vernon Press
1000 N West Street, Suite 1200
Wilmington, Delaware, 19801
United States

In the rest of the world:
Vernon Press
C/Sancti Espiritu 17,
Malaga, 29006
Spain

Series in Literary Studies

Library of Congress Control Number: 2020943385

ISBN: 978-1-64889-229-5

Also available: 978-1-64889-015-4 [Hardback]; 978-1-64889-092-5 [PDF, E-Book]

Product and company names mentioned in this work are the trademarks of their respective owners. While every care has been taken in preparing this work, neither the authors nor Vernon Art and Science Inc. may be held responsible for any loss or damage caused or alleged to be caused directly or indirectly by the information contained in it.

Every effort has been made to trace all copyright holders, but if any have been inadvertently overlooked the publisher will be pleased to include any necessary credits in any subsequent reprint or edition.

Cover design by Vernon Press. Cover image: Emily Dickinson Collection, Amherst College Archives & Special Collections.

Table of Contents

List of Tables — v

List of Figures — v

Acknowledgments — vii

Introduction — ix

Chapter 1 **Dickinson's Breath of Life** — 1
Cynthia L. Hallen
Brigham Young University

    Abstract — 1
    Emily Dickinson and Noah Webster's Collocations — 4
    A Digital Account of Emily Dickinson's Nouns — 7
    Emily Dickinson's Person Names — 10
    Emily Dickinson's Kennings — 14
    Metonymy in Emily Dickinson's Verse — 16
    Love, Light, and the Breath of Life — 17
    Appendix A — 19
    Appendix B — 38
    Appendix C — 47
    Appendix D — 51
    Works Cited — 61
    Further Reading — 62

Chapter 2 **"Syllables of Velvet, Sentences of Plush": Emily Dickinson as Polyglot** — 65
Nicole Panizza
Coventry University

    Abstract — 65
    Spatial Improvisations – Emily Dickinson's
      "Lyric Communications" — 68
    Dickinson's Music Training — 68
    Dickinson's Music-Making in the Home — 75
    Bilingual Practice — 79
    "In adequate Music there is a Major and a Minor" — 85

	"I can improvise better at night" – Emily Dickinson's "riffs"	94
	Works Cited	98
Chapter 3	**The Notorious E.E.D.: Rap in the Poems of Emily Dickinson** Holly Norton *University of Northwestern Ohio*	101
	Abstract	101
	Works Cited	116
Chapter 4	**"Some seek in Art –": Language and Literary Influence in Fascicle 30** Trisha Kannan *Independent Scholar*	119
	Abstract	119
	What Are the Fascicles?	120
	Fascicle 30 and Literary Influence	126
	Sheet Four: Immortal Poets and Sources of Inspiration	132
	Sheet Five: Poems of Nature and Experience	134
	Sheet Six: The Power of Pain	136
	Sheet One: Nature's Ephemeral Beauty	139
	Sheet Two: Poetic Inspiration and the Power of Language	140
	Sheet Three: The Power of Failure	143
	Conclusion	144
	Works Cited	145
	Further Reading	147
Index		149

Table of Contents

List of Tables   v

List of Figures   v

Acknowledgments   vii

Introduction   ix

Chapter 1   **Dickinson's Breath of Life**   1
Cynthia L. Hallen
Brigham Young University

     Abstract   1
     Emily Dickinson and Noah Webster's Collocations   4
     A Digital Account of Emily Dickinson's Nouns   7
     Emily Dickinson's Person Names   10
     Emily Dickinson's Kennings   14
     Metonymy in Emily Dickinson's Verse   16
     Love, Light, and the Breath of Life   17
     Appendix A   19
     Appendix B   38
     Appendix C   47
     Appendix D   51
     Works Cited   61
     Further Reading   62

Chapter 2   **"Syllables of Velvet, Sentences of Plush":
Emily Dickinson as Polyglot**   65
Nicole Panizza
Coventry University

     Abstract   65
     Spatial Improvisations – Emily Dickinson's
        "Lyric Communications"   68
     Dickinson's Music Training   68
     Dickinson's Music-Making in the Home   75
     Bilingual Practice   79
     "In adequate Music there is a Major and a Minor"   85

| | "I can improvise better at night" – Emily Dickinson's "riffs" | 94 |
| | Works Cited | 98 |

| Chapter 3 | **The Notorious E.E.D.: Rap in the Poems of Emily Dickinson** | 101 |

Holly Norton
University of Northwestern Ohio

| | Abstract | 101 |
| | Works Cited | 116 |

| Chapter 4 | **"Some seek in Art –": Language and Literary Influence in Fascicle 30** | 119 |

Trisha Kannan
Independent Scholar

	Abstract	119
	What Are the Fascicles?	120
	Fascicle 30 and Literary Influence	126
	Sheet Four: Immortal Poets and Sources of Inspiration	132
	Sheet Five: Poems of Nature and Experience	134
	Sheet Six: The Power of Pain	136
	Sheet One: Nature's Ephemeral Beauty	139
	Sheet Two: Poetic Inspiration and the Power of Language	140
	Sheet Three: The Power of Failure	143
	Conclusion	144
	Works Cited	145
	Further Reading	147

Index 149

List of Tables

Table 1.3 Top 50 High-Frequency Nouns Occurring in Dickinson's Poems and Letters   7

Table 1.4 Most Frequent Person Name Headwords by Categories and Examples   11

Table 1.5 Most Frequent Proper Nouns by Number of Occurrences in Dickinson's Poems   12

Table 1.1 Catalogue of Emily Dickinson's Quoted Material   19

Table 1.2 Sample of Emily Dickinson's Language Features   38

Table 1.6 Sample of Emily Dickinson's Kennings   47

Table 1.7 Sample of Emily Dickinson's Metonymies   51

List of Figures

Figure 2.1 EDR 469. Houghton Library, Harvard University. "Di Tanti Palpiti" with variations, Edward L. White – Bars 1-10.   83

Figure 2.2 EDR 469. Houghton Library, Harvard University. Kreutzer's "Overture to Lodoiska," arr. By Charles Czerny (piano duet) – Secondo, Bars 18-32.   83

Figure 2.3 "We talked with each other about each other," in Emily Dickinson Collection, Box 6, Folder 52, Amherst College Archives and Special Collections, Amherst College Library   84

Acknowledgments

This collection would not exist without the expertise, patience, and generosity of Emily Seelbinder, professor emerita of English and Creative Writing at Queens University of Charlotte. The editors are tremendously grateful for the time and effort she dedicated to preparing these essays for publication. The editors would also like to thank the Emily Dickinson International Society (EDIS), which has been a steady source of inspiration, support, and collegiality for years. Much of the scholarship the writers relied on to produce these essays stems from EDIS members, many of whom have become mentors, colleagues, and friends after so many annual meetings and conferences, always filled with lively debates and discussions and a shared love of all things Emily Dickinson. Finally, the editors recognize the important contribution of the South Atlantic Modern Language Association (SAMLA). The idea for a collection exploring the language of Emily Dickinson derived from a 2019 panel on the subject, and SAMLA's conference organizers always work tirelessly to create an inclusive, collaborative environment to promote diverse scholarship that is accessible and available to a wider audience.

I would also like to thank Dr. Robyn Bell, whose course on Dickinson's fascicles during my time as an undergraduate in the College of Creative Studies at UC Santa Barbara changed my life. Prior to Dr. Bell's class, I had an image in my head of Dickinson as a hoarder of poems; her texts were so difficult because they were akin to conversations Dickinson was having with herself. I did not know about the fascicles, nor did I know that she circulated hundreds of poems with her letters. I had never conceived of attending graduate school until that class, and then I could not imagine doing anything else. At the time, Dr. Bell knew much more about academia than I did, and she expressed concern that graduate school would "ruin" Dickinson for me, which very nearly was the case. But the people at EDIS revived and sustained me, particularly Eleanor Heginbotham, Alexandra Socarides, Martha Nell Smith, and Emily Seelbinder. Marianne Noble and Dan Manheim spent considerable time offering feedback on an early version of my Fascicle 30 essay, and I am eternally grateful. As Martha Ackmann writes in *These Fevered Days: Ten Pivotal Moments in the Making of Emily Dickinson*, "There is no doubt she is a towering poetic voice. But there's something else about her too. Emily Dickinson reminds us what it's like to be alive" (xxiii). The goal of this collection is to clarify Dickinson's language, yet her allure goes beyond writing memorable, captivating, powerful poems; there is something indescribable and indecipherable about her work that calls to us and keeps us coming back for more.

Introduction

This collection brings together renowned and independent scholars who are captivated by the ways in which Emily Dickinson used words. The authors revel in the difficulty of her language, in its component parts, its visceral effects, its sounds and flavors. The essays delve into a variety of subjects centered around how Dickinson manipulated language, providing fresh insight and new ways of thinking about a poet who has been at the center of the American literary canon for more than a century. One need not be a Dickinson expert to appreciate this collection, however. The writers translate Dickinson's difficulty into language that is accessible and informative for advanced scholars and general readers alike.

Cynthia L. Hallen, associate professor of linguistics at Brigham Young University and creator of the invaluable *Emily Dickinson Lexicon*, opens the collection with her essay "Dickinson's Breath of Life." An in-depth exploration of Dickinson's language features, this chapter seeks to explain how Dickinson's linguistic choices created such powerful poems. Hallen analyzes the role of direct quotation, lexical collocates, nouns, person names, kennings, and metonymy in Dickinson's work. The result is a better understanding of how Dickinson achieved her goal of creating living verses that breathe vital light and love into all who read them.

Nicole Panizza, distinguished pianist and assistant professor of music at Coventry University, explores Dickinson's relationship to music in "'Syllables of Velvet, Sentences of Plush': Emily Dickinson as Polyglot." Exploring Dickinson's musical background and deciphering the pivotal place of music in Dickinson's artistic process as only a musician could, Panizza argues that Dickinson is a polyglot, a person with knowledge of and the ability to move between multiple languages. Dickinson was not an "industry professional," of course, but she was an accomplished pianist with a deep affinity for the sounds, sensations, and understanding that only music could bring. Panizza also provides a fascinating look at the intersections between Dickinson and jazz, detailing how contemporary musicians find inspiration in Dickinson's work.

Holly Norton, author of the poetry collection *Letting Go* and professor of English at the University of Northwestern Ohio, explores the connections between nineteenth-century poetry and twentieth-century rap lyrics in "The Notorious E.E.D.: Rap in the Poems of Emily Dickinson." Norton focuses on the work of the Notorious B.I.G. and Tupac to show thematic similarities to Dickinson regarding death, the afterlife, and the power of poetry. Norton recognizes the disparities in the lives of Dickinson and rappers such as the

Notorious B.I.G. and Tupac, but her articulation of the ways in which their poetic ideas intersect provides an enlightening new way of thinking about the poetry of Emily Dickinson and the transcendent power of language.

Trisha Kannan, writer, editor, and independent scholar, contributes to the growing body of fascicle scholarship in "'Some seek in Art –': Language and Literary Influence in Fascicle 30." By closely analyzing the poems Dickinson placed in Fascicle 30, Kannan locates specific correlations to the work of John Keats that have remained unexamined. In particular, Kannan explores how the fascicle contains "echoes," to borrow Elizabeth Petrino's apt term, of several of Keats's poems, including "Nature and the Poets," "Fancy," "Fairy Song," "Bards of Passion and of Mirth," "Ode to a Nightingale," and "To Autumn." Observing these echoes reveals thematic strains that Dickinson shared with Keats about the power of art, poetic inspiration, and the joyful and painful events of human life.

Following the approach of Dickinson editors and scholarship of the past few decades, this collection renders Dickinson's manuscripts into print without too much editorial intrusion, which means Dickinson's misspellings and grammatical errors have been left as they are without the addition of *sic*. The editors believe Dickinson does not need to be "fixed" and that her poetry simply wouldn't be the same if she had not decided that "upon" should be spelled "opon."

Chapter 1

Dickinson's Breath of Life

Cynthia L. Hallen
Brigham Young University

Abstract

Emily Dickinson lived in the noon of a philological renaissance that inspired several nineteenth-century scholars and authors to think of human language as an organic manifestation of human life. Her awareness of the life of language is apparent in the first letter she sent to Thomas Wentworth Higginson, in which she asked: "Are you too deeply occupied to say if my Verse is alive?" (L260, 15 April 1862). This essay documents how the poet's verses are alive lexically and semantically. Scholars have explored Dickinson's style, grammar, biblical allusions, classical strategies, cognitive patterns, elliptical constructions, and rhetorical figures. This essay considers additional language features that enable Dickinson's words to breathe distinctly, including collocations, etymologies, merisms, kennings, pairs, proper nouns, quoted material, word frequencies, and webplays between Dickinson's diction and Noah Webster's dictionary.

Key words: philology, language features, webplay

***

Emily Dickinson lived in the noon of a philological renaissance that inspired several nineteenth-century scholars to think of human language as a vital and living manifestation of Nature. In an 1851 essay on the distinction of words, English philologist Richard C. Trench wrote that words have "a body and a soul." Scholars like Trench believed that human language developed in an "organic" way and that the tree of language was a natural outgrowth of word roots (Gura 117–118). The organic image of language as a living tree growing up from life-giving word roots influenced New England literary authors and poets (Gura 138–141), including Henry David Thoreau, Walt Whitman, and Emily Dickinson. Thoreau wrote that a written word "is the work of art nearest to life itself" that may not "only be read but actually breathed from all human lips" (355). Whitman wrote that the etymology of words is "the history of Nature . . . and of the organic Universe;" he believed that words become vitalized "in the mind that enters on their study" (572). In one of her verses, Dickinson asserted that a word "begins to live" when it is spoken (Fr278),[1] and in another poem she wrote that "a Vital Word / Came all the way from Life to me" (Fr996).

Emily Dickinson's awareness of the vitality of language is apparent throughout her poems and letters. In the first letter she sent to scholar Thomas W. Higginson, she asked, "Are you too deeply occupied to say if my Verse is alive?" (L260, 15 April 1862). She continued that if Higginson were to reply that her words "breathed," her gratitude would be "quick," an adjective that Noah Webster defined as "living" in the etymological sense and "speedy" in the derivative sense.[2] For Dickinson, words were vibrant and immediate; they had "an existence, a power, an autonomy of their own" (Sewall 77). More than 150 years later, scholars such as Erika Scheurer attest to the immediacy of language in Dickinson's poetry. Her poems are still alive with words that breathe "distinctly" because of the "Cohesive" language choices in her "loved Philology" (Fr1715).

Dickinson would have learned about the importance of living language as a student in the Classical track at Amherst Academy. In his rhetoric textbook, Samuel Newman explained that a good writing style depends on the quality of "vivacity" and declared that a "happy choice of words" is the key to achieving liveliness in language (164). Newman elaborated on effective word choice, stating that vivacity implies that "thoughts are exhibited with distinctness before the mind of the reader" (164). Writers may achieve vivacity by using "specific" words and phrases that "convey a more full and distinct meaning to the mind" than that which is conveyed by generic terms (164). He went on to identify several more strategies for achieving vivacity: language figures, unusual word orders, elliptical omissions, special sentence structures, verb tense changes, and direct quotations in narration (165–178).

Whether intentionally or instinctively, Dickinson employed many of Newman's vivacious language strategies in her poetry. For example, she incorporated direct quotation of published materials into the fabric of her verse, and she used seven kinds of quotations for various functions: to punctuate dialogue, to show emphasis, to highlight figurative usage, to foreground humor, to identify literary allusions, to mark names, and to quote herself. Dickinson used single or double quotation marks in 223 out of 1,789 poems; the usage is most frequent in her earlier poems from 1850–1862. The most frequent function of quotation marks was for direct quotation of literary works, many of which are Biblical allusions. The second-highest category of quotation usage was for dialogue, and the third-highest was for emphasizing a

---

[1] See also L379.
[2] *Emily Dickinson Lexicon* (EDL), http://edl.byu.edu/webster/term/1301652.

word or phrase in the text. Table 1.1 provides a listing of 389 quotations in Dickinson's poems by poem number, function, source, and year (see Appendix A).[3] These quotations contribute to vivacity in Dickinson's language by creating an impression of multiple voices and personas.

Over the past 50 years, scholarly approaches to Dickinson's language have been extensive and diverse. Language topics range from Howard's 1957 treatment of vocabulary, to Lindberg-Seyersted's 1968 book on stylistic features, to Cuddy's 1978 article on the influence of Latin studies, to Burbick's 1982 essay on pronoun references, to Budick's 1985 study of symbolic poetics, to Miller's 1987 book on grammar, to Small's 1990 treatise on rhyme, to Hagenbüchle's comprehensive 1993 article on language heritage, to Sharon-Zisser's 1994 essay on similes, to Freeman's 1995 cognitive treatment of metaphors, to Bennett's 1997 inventory of Biblical allusions, to Ross's 2001 elucidation of prosody patterns, to Monte's 2003 discussion of reading philologically, to Hamilton's 2005 study of the function of figures, and to Hubbard's 2014 fascicle analysis of word variants.

Suzanne Juhasz's 2000 exposition on the role of analogy as a linguistic master-trope for the poet is especially illuminating because it advances the role of "psychodynamic" repetition in Dickinson's writing. Juhasz posits that Dickinson felt "an irresistible compulsion to repeat, in forms of repetition that are re-creative, even transformative" (24). Re-creative repetition makes sense as a key to understanding Dickinson's language because human language is a dynamic interplay of repetitions and variations in phonetic, morphological, syntactic, lexical, semantic, and pragmatic frames. Dickinson chose to foreground marked repetitions and variations of language at all linguistic levels in order to make her verses remarkable, memorable, beautiful, and alive. Table 1.2 is a compilation of 60 distinctive language features that contribute to the vivacity, vitality, animation, activity, liveliness, and longevity of Dickinson's writing (see Appendix B).[4] This essay focuses on additional ways the words and phrases in Dickinson's work are lexically alive and semantically vital, and I examine the language features that enable Dickinson's words to breathe distinctly, including Webster collocations, noun frequencies, person names, and kennings.

---

[3] Special thanks to my former research assistant Stanley Thayne, who compiled the quotations table under my direction.
[4] See http://edl.byu.edu/webster/term/2371707.

Emily Dickinson and Noah Webster's Collocations

Language connections between Emily Dickinson's poetry and Noah Webster's dictionary are supported by historical and biographical contexts. Emily Elizabeth Dickinson attended school with Emily Elizabeth Fowler Ford, Webster's granddaughter. Webster had lived in Amherst from 1812–1822 as he worked on the first edition of his 1828 *American Dictionary of the English Language* (ADEL). During those 10 years, he helped establish Amherst College and Amherst Academy with Samuel Fowler Dickinson, Emily's grandfather.[5] In 1844, Samuel's son Edward Dickinson purchased a copy of Webster's dictionary for his daughter Emily's fourteenth birthday. This 1844 reprint of the 1841 edition of the ADEL, published by J.S. & C. Adams Brothers in Amherst, had an appendix of the last words that Webster worked on before his death in 1843. Dickinson's brother Austin recalled seeing "Webster's big dictionary" on the kitchen table, where Emily was often at work in their home (Sewall 12). Martha Dickinson Bianchi reported that her aunt Emily read the dictionary "as a priest his breviary," or book of daily devotions (80). In a second letter to her mentor, Dickinson told Higginson that for several years her "Lexicon" had been her only companion (L261, 25 April 1862). In Webster's 1844 lexicon, Dickinson could feast on over 82,764 alphabetized entries that provided living language for her unique poetic diction.

As "a lexicon-loving writer" (Eberwein 35), Dickinson studied Webster's dictionary and used material in its entries to enhance language choices in her work.[6] Therefore, readers of Dickinson can benefit when they use Webster's 1844 dictionary to enhance their understanding of her poems. For example, identifying lexical collocates (neighbors) is one of the best ways to determine the meaning of words in a poem because such collocates create cohesion in the text. This semantic networking is especially helpful because of the syntactic compactions and grammatical elisions that Dickinson employs in much of her work (Steiner 368). Although a semantic connection between words in a Dickinson poem may not be directly attributable to Webster's ADEL, its entries can document subtle cohesive ties, and those ties can help readers more fully understand and interpret the poet's textual relations.

Using a WordCruncher computer concordance program,[7] my research team identified lexical combinations in Webster's 1844 dictionary that may have

---

[5] See Katherine Garland's "Noah Webster's House" and "Emily Dickinson's Schooling: Amherst Academy."

[6] See, for example, Willis J. Buckingham's "Emily Dickinson's Dictionary" and Richard Benvenuto's "Words Within Words: Dickinson's Use of the Dictionary."

[7] See https://wordcruncher.com/.

influenced the poetic compositions of Emily Dickinson.[8] We coined the term "webplay" to describe these sets of corresponding content words.[9] A webplay occurs when the words used to define an entry in Webster's dictionary correspond with a similar set of words in one or more of Dickinson's poems. We have identified several kinds of webplay correspondences:

In **simple webplay**, one content word in a Dickinson poem corresponds to one other word in a Webster 1844 headword entry. For example, definition four of Webster's entry for the intransitive verb RETURN[10] says, "To come again; to revisit."[11] Dickinson's poem "Alone and in a Circumstance" includes the clauses "Revisiting my late abode . . . I can return the Blow" (Fr1174).

In **multiple webplay**, word correspondences in a Webster headword entry occur in more than one Dickinson poem. For example, Webster's 1844 entry for the noun DOUBT includes the phrase "defect of knowledge."[12] Dickinson uses forms of "doubt" and "knowledge" together in several poems. The diction of the poem "I have a Bird in spring" (Fr4) includes Knowing, doubting, and doubt. The poems "Delayed till she had ceased to know" (Fr67) and "What we see we know somewhat" (Fr1272) also include the juxtaposition of know and doubtful. The poem "Who were 'the Father and the Son'" (Fr1280) likewise includes doubtless and know.

With **complex webplay**, more than one content word in a Dickinson poem corresponds to more than one content word in a Webster headword entry. For example, definition one of Webster's entry for the transitive verb REVEAL says, "To disclose; . . . to make known something before unknown or concealed; as, to reveal secrets."[13] Likewise, stanza two of Dickinson's poem "The Lightning is a yellow Fork" (Fr1140) is cohesively sealed with the words disclosed, concealed, and revealed.

With **collocational webplay**, words in close proximity (word neighbors) in a Dickinson poem also appear in close proximity in a corresponding Webster headword entry. Definition two of Webster's entry for the adjective RIGHT says, "That alone is right in the sight of God, which is consonant to his will or law;

---

[8] Special thanks to my research assistant Mel Wilson, who collaborated with me on the study of Dickinson's webplay. Thanks also to other former students who have contributed to my research on Dickinson's language.

[9] Content words are nouns, verbs, adjectives, and adverbs that carry meaning semantically in a language, whereas, function words are conjunctions, prepositions, interjections, determiners, and pronouns that enable grammatical relations.

[10] Underlining added to mark the corresponding items.

[11] See http://edl.byu.edu/webster/term/2382637.

[12] See http://edl.byu.edu/webster/term/2427003.

[13] See http://edl.byu.edu/webster/term/2382662.

this being the only <u>perfect</u> standard of <u>truth</u> and justice."[14] Stanzas six and seven of Dickinson's "Fitter to see Him, I may be" (Fr834) include the words <u>right</u>, <u>perfect</u>, <u>sight</u>, and <u>Truth</u>.

A comprehensive lexicon analysis of the words BELIEF and BELIEVE in Dickinson's poems may yield insights about how she explored life through poetic language. In several poems, Dickinson uses belief as a synonym for faith, or trust in God. "These are the days when birds come back" (Fr122) includes a webplay of the words "belief," "witness," and "Permit." Webster's etymology of the noun BELIEF includes the glosses "leave, license, <u>permission</u>," so to "believe" is to <u>permit</u> or allow that something may be plausible. Dickinson's word "witness" occurs in Webster's entry for the noun BELIEF under definition one: "an assent of mind to the truth of a declaration, proposition, or alleged fact, on the ground of evidence, distinct from personal knowledge; as the *belief* of the gospel; *belief* of a <u>witness</u>." The lexical webplay link between the word "belief" and "witness" in "These are the days" is confirmed by a sound play pun on the word "leaf" at the end of the fourth verse. A "timid <u>leaf</u>" is a testimony of the be<u>lief</u> that spring will come again and life will be renewed. The dance of falling <u>leaves</u> is a witness to one who be<u>lieves</u> that the dead will be resurrected.

Dickinson repeats the sound play between "leaves" and "believes" as well as the webplay between "witnesses" and "believes" in the poem "Her face was in a bed of hair" (Fr1755), a portrait of a woman who is dying. The woman's face already reflects the pending realities of the cemetery plot, and her voice is more gentle than "the tune that totters in the leaves." The sound of her voice, like the wind in the trees, may not induce one to believe in God, but seeing firsthand the woman's spiritual transition from life to death is conducive to belief: "Who hears may be incredulous, / Who <u>witnesses</u>, <u>believes</u>." In this poem, a metaphor for belief emerges. Mortals cannot yet see God, but they can see the effect of his work throughout creation. Such sentiments were popular among Dickinson's contemporaries in nineteenth-century Victorian poetry, as seen in Christina Rossetti's poem:

> Who has seen the wind?
>   Neither I nor you:
> But when the leaves hang trembling
>   The wind is passing thro'.
> Who has seen the wind?
>   Neither you nor I:
> But when the trees bow down their heads
>   The wind is passing by. (93)

---

[14] See http://edl.byu.edu/webster/term/2383035.

We cannot see the wind, but we can hear the tune of the wind tottering in the leaves. Believing in God is like seeing the effects of the wind in the trees, or like witnessing the effects of belief in the transfigured face of a dying woman.

A Digital Account of Emily Dickinson's Nouns

Nouns, as a major lexical category, are the lifeblood of Emily Dickinson's language. A comparison of the top 50 high-frequency nouns in the entire corpus of Webster's 1844 dictionary and a database of Dickinson's collected poems yields a correlation of nine lexical items: **day, God, hand, house, man, name, place, thing, time**.[15] Eight of the nine high-frequency words that Webster and Dickinson share are also among the high-frequency words found in Shakespeare's collected works and in the King James Bible. From a big-data lexical standpoint, Dickinson's most frequent nouns appear to be representative of universal semantic themes prevalent in the literature of the English language since the sixteenth-century Renaissance.

One may ask, "Why focus on nouns?" or "What is the significance of high-frequency nouns?" A simple answer is that nouns express the semantic themes of human language and show us major motifs in an author's ontogeny. Bryan Short explains that the "theory of linguistic origination and growth available to Dickinson almost universally gives primacy to nouns over other parts of speech" (110). Nouns act as subjects or objects that carry the weight of meaning in written texts and in spoken discourses (Werning 67). Noun subjects serve as agents or actors in the "basic drama of every sentence" (Becker 187), and noun objects are patients or recipients of verbal action in the semantic staging of thoughts through the medium of words.

Table 1.3 shows a compilation of the top 50 high-frequency nouns in Dickinson's poems and letters, in descending order for each corpus, with ellipses indicating inflections such as "s" plural and "'s" possessive forms.

Table 1.3 Top 50 High-Frequency Nouns Occurring in Dickinson's Poems and Letters

Frequency	Dickinson Poem Nouns	Frequency	Dickinson Letter Nouns
291	day, days, day's	713	love, loves, love's
208	life ...	621	friend ...
196	sun	530	home ...

---

[15] Word-count data is based on the 1955 Johnson variorum edition of Emily Dickinson's poems in a WordCruncher concordance database authorized by Harvard University Press.

185	man ...		489	day ...	
182	eye ...		488	time ...	
175	bird ...		406	father ...	
171	time ...		384	hope ...	
170	face ...		381	letter ...	
161	heaven		318	mother ...	
160	nature		296	thought ...	
160	way ...		292	heart ...	
156	death ...		270	life ...	
151	God ...		242	thing ...	
148	heart ...		239	sister ...	
148	summer ...		215	night ...	
147	night ...		208	week ...	
142	soul ...		206	morning ...	
136	morning ...		174	evening ...	
136	sea ...		173	flower ...	
120	bee ...		171	world ...	
116	feet ...		167	word ...	
116	flower ...		165	hand ...	
116	thing ...		165	summer ...	
115	hand ...		158	child ...	
113	sky ...		158	way ...	
96	love ...		157	bird ...	
94	home ...		156	eye ...	
93	house ...		153	God, gods ...	
90	noon		153	year ...	
89	light ...		147	house ...	
89	wind ...		142	mind ...	
89	world ...		131	heaven ...	
83	door ...		131	man ...	
83	year ...		130	face ...	
81	place ...		128	nothing ...	
78	hill ...		121	note ...	

78	mind …		119	spring …
71	friend …		119	trust
68	star …		114	girl …
66	grave …		107	Doctor …
66	tree		107	hour …
65	child …		101	spirit …
64	air …		100	moment …
64	grace …		98	death …
63	earth …		96	brother …
62	name …		95	cousin …
60	snow …		94	door …
59	eternity …		94	school …
59	pain …		93	name …
59	paradise		90	place …

The shaded cells reveal a correlation of 29 high-frequency nouns common to the poems and letters that Dickinson wrote throughout her lifetime: **bird, child, day, death, door, eye, face, flower, friend, God, hand, heart, heaven, home, house, life, love, man, mind, morning, name, night, place, summer, thing, time, way, world, year** (bold added).

Many of the top 50 poem-nouns listed in the left column occur in Dickinson's first attested poem, "Awake ye muses nine, sing me a strain divine" (Fr1). This 1850 valentine steps out like a debutante in front of the entire poetic corpus, decked with anticipatory nouns that presage prospective themes: **air, bee, bird, day, death, earth, eye, flower, God, heaven, home, life, morn, night, sea, soul, sun, thing, time, tree, wind, world**. Such corpus theme observations are not new nor trivial. A 1980 article by Lucy Brashear asserts that Emily Dickinson's first extant poem should be regarded as a prototype and valued as "the earliest record of the imagery and themes which inform her later work" (98). Using "the Dickinson concordance," Brashear documents that certain "nature terms—flower, wind, air, earth, moon, jewel, and bird—are among her most consistently used vocabulary" (93). The frequency of these terms is even higher, she explains, if we consider synonym or hyponym variations of these concepts in the poetic corpus, such as birds as robins, sparrows, crows, or hummingbirds.

From a pre-digital perspective, Brashear had noticed three distinct groupings in the prototype valentine: terms for religion, nature, and mankind. Her categories hold up well from a digital perspective in the top 50 nouns that occur frequently throughout Dickinson's poems (see Table 1.3). Brashear posits a "religion" grouping that is evident in the terms **eternity, God, grace, heaven, life, light, love, soul, paradise**. A "nature" group is observable in the terms **air, bee, bird, day, earth, flower, hill, life, light, morning, nature, night, noon, place, sea, summer, sky, sun, wind, world, snow, star, tree**. A group of "mankind" terms is manifest in **child, death, door, eyes, face, feet, friend, grave, hand, heart, home, house, life, love, man, mind, name, pain**. Terms such as **life** and **light** pertain to all three groups, while abstract terms such as **thing, time,** and **way** are hard to categorize, but a holistic lexical analysis validates at least three distinct groupings.

Brashear links her three groupings to five themes "which are closely associated with Dickinson's poetry and life—love, marriage, death, loneliness, and melancholy" (95). In a discussion of these themes, Brashear reads the lighthearted love poem as an ironic omen of Dickinson's life-long monomaniac infatuation with death. However, from a data point of view, I have found that Dickinson's top 50 poem-nouns tend to be semantically neutral or positive for the most part. Only three of Dickinson's 50 nouns are obviously negative by general definition: **death, grave, pain**. In spite of tabloid diagnoses and scholarly stereotypes, Emily Dickinson was actually a very happy person, according to a 1932 news feature story on a lecture by her niece Martha Dickinson Bianchi: "The deep spirituality of this modest writer of simple yet mystical verses was brought out by Mme. Bianchi in several anecdotes about her aunt. . . . Despite her mystic nature, the New England poet had a happy disposition."[16] When tested with digital tools and firsthand biographical accounts, rumors of Dickinson's melancholy obsession with death prove to be greatly exaggerated.

Emily Dickinson's Person Names

Proper nouns, including the names of living or once-living persons, contribute to the vitality of Emily Dickinson's language. Person names are specific appellations for unique individuals, characters, and personified entities. In her poems, Dickinson uses 140 different person names, also known as "anthroponyms" in the field of onomastics. The capitalized names of people and personified entities appear in 221 of the 1,789 poems in the Franklin edition, about 12% of the poetic corpus. The person names appear as early as the first poem in 1850 (Fr1) and as late as 1885, the year before Dickinson's death (Fr1776). In other words, the person names are distributed throughout the poems and are not confined to one particular time period.

---

[16] Newspaper clipping, Dickinson-Bianchi archives, Special Collections, Brown University.

Dickinson's 140 person names fall into 10 basic pragmatic categories as listed and exemplified in Table 1.4:

Table 1.4 Most Frequent Person Name Headwords by Categories and Examples

Pragmatic Categories	Number of Headwords	Person Name Examples
Biblical	38	Abraham, Jehovah, Nicodemus
Historical	21	Cato, Elizabeth, Essex, Soto
Domestic	18	Austin, Carlo, Katie, Shaw
Literary	16	Cinderella, Hamlet, Trotwood
Authors	11	Bronte, Dante, Sophocles
Mythological	10	Jupiter, Orpheus
Astronomy	8	Herschel, Orion
Religious	7	Druid, Jesuit
Nature	6	Bartsia, Epigea, Phebe
Fine Arts	5	Guido, Mozart, Titian
Total:	**140**	

The Biblical names category includes terms for Deity, as well as people featured in the Old Testament and the New Testament. Historical names range from classical allusions to nineteenth-century references, from the Old World to the New World. The Domestic category refers to Dickinson's family, friends, neighbors, and her dog Carlo. The Literary category includes characters from plays, novels, and folk authors. The Authors category includes classical writers, British writers, one Italian writer, and one North American author. The Mythological category includes Greek and Roman deities as well as classical heroes. The Astronomy category consists of scientists and personified heavenly bodies. The Religious category counts person names pertaining to the divine that do not fit into the Biblical and Mythological categories. The Nature category features several plants and one bird, while the Fine Arts category features painters and one musician.

Semantic and social concepts identified in the 10 pragmatic categories show the importance of certain themes in Dickinson's poetic diction, as well as in nineteenth-century New England language and culture. The 38 person names in the Biblical category contribute the greatest number of headwords, more than one-fourth of the 140 person names. Historical person names form a second tier of thematic emphasis, followed by Domestic person names as a third tier.

Of the 221 poems that include onomastic entities, 172 have only one person name, 32 poems have two, eight poems have three, two poems have four, three poems have five, and the two earliest Dickinson poems have eight person names each. Multiple person names from the 10 pragmatic categories appear early in the poems. The eight person names in Dickinson's 1850 valentine "Awake ye muses nine" (Fr1) include three Biblical headwords ("God," "Adam," "Eve") and five Domestic schoolmate headwords ("Sarah," "Eliza," "Emeline," "Harriet," "Susan"). The eight person names in her 1852 valentine "Sic transit gloria mundi" (Fr2) fall into a variety of categories: Author ("Peter Parley"); Historical ("Daniel Boon," "Columbus"); Domestic ("Peter," "Pattie"); Biblical ("Adam"); and Astronomy ("Luna," "Mars").

Person names in the Biblical category have the highest number of overall occurrences throughout Emily Dickinson's poems. The total number of tokens, meaning repeated instances of the 140 unique onomastic entities, throughout all of the poems is 395 person names. Of the 395 total occurrences of person names, 260 are instances of Biblical headwords. Table 1.5 shows that the headword "God" occurs more times and in more poems than any other person name in Dickinson's poetry. The title "Lord" ranks second, followed by the name "Jesus," and then the titles "Christ" and "Savior":

Table 1.5 Most Frequent Proper Nouns by Number of Occurrences in Dickinson's Poems

Person Name Headword	Pragmatic Category	# of Occurrences
God	Biblical	135
Lord	Biblical	22
Jesus	Biblical	20
Christ	Biblical	11
Savior	Biblical	8
Gabriel	Biblical	7
Adam	Biblical	6
Jehovah	Biblical	6
Moses	Biblical	6

The top five person names in Emily Dickinson's poetry are appellations for God the Father and God the Son in the Bible. The next four most frequent person names are also Biblical. As in other early nineteenth-century New England communities, people in Dickinson's hometown of Amherst, Massachusetts, were animated by religious inquiry. Dickinson's language reflects that hunger for spiritual enlightenment. The numerous Biblical person names suggest that

Dickinson is indeed a Christian poet, in the tradition of earlier truth-seekers and metaphysical poets, such as Hildegard von Bingen, Sor Juana Inés de la Cruz, John Donne, and George Herbert. Emily Dickinson may have challenged accepted notions of God and questioned religious practices, but she certainly does not ignore them.

Careful attention to the literal and figurative meaning of person names can help readers interpret the semantic possibilities that contribute to the vitality of a Dickinson poem. For example, two poems employ the person name "Cato," and each occurrence has literal and figurative senses:[17]

Cato (-'s), proper n. [L. *catus*, sharp, shrewd, cunning.]

- A. Marcus Porcius Cato (95–46 B.C.); Cato the younger; vocal opponent to Caesar; Roman politician, orator, and military hero; uncle of Brutus; father of Portia; protagonist of a dramatic tragedy that Joseph Addison wrote in 1712; [fig.] a persuasive speech maker; a stoic orator; a lecturing moralist.
  Fr76 My flowers ... eloquent declare / What Cato couldn't prove me

- B. Senator; congressman; representative; [fig.] Edward Dickinson; Massachusetts statesman; father of Emily Dickinson; [metaphor] God; Father in Heaven; higher power in nature and the universe.
  Fr149 Great Caesar! Condescend / The Daisy, to receive, / Gathered by Cato's Daughter, / With your majestic leave!

In the poem "The rainbow never tells me" (Fr76), the proper name "Cato" can refer to the historical figure, Addison's main character adapted from the historical person, or any eloquent speaker. In the poem "Great Caesar" (Fr149), Dickinson uses "Cato" to refer to any congressman, to her own father who served as a congressman, or to God the Father who serves as the most ancient "Senator" of the universe. The phrase "Cato's Daughter" thus can refer to Emily herself, as the daughter of Edward Dickinson and as a daughter of Deity, as well as to Portia, the historical daughter of Cato, who was the wife of the assassin Brutus in the days of Julius Caesar.

Dickinson's classical education at Amherst Academy and Mount Holyoke Female Seminary may have provided a more general definition of the phrase "proper name" than the one to which contemporary readers are accustomed. Traditionally, proper names such as names for a particular person are marked typographically with a capital letter in standard English texts. Dickinson does

---

[17] See http://edl.byu.edu/lexicon/term/632063.

capitalize all of the person names in her poems. However, she sometimes capitalizes common names that refer to people, places, or things in general, so distinguishing between person names and common names in the poems can require extra effort. For example, we originally thought that the capitalized form "Crashe" was a person name in the poem "Crumbling is not an instant's Act" (Fr1010). We spent some time looking for the scientist responsible for "Crashe's law." To our amusement, we learned that "Crashe" was Dickinson's idiosyncratic spelling of the common noun "crash," and it is not a person name.[18]

Emily Dickinson's Kennings

Dickinson's poetry is alive not only because she created new songs by innovation but because she was well versed in traditional semantic themes and syntactic formulas. In his 1995 book *How to Kill a Dragon*, Harvard scholar Calvert Watkins identified several formulaic phrase types that appear frequently in poetic texts that belong to the Indo-European language family tradition. Watkins's poetic formulas fall into two basic categories: 1) simple formulas, such as synonymous and antithetical word pairs, that function as symbolic signs for totality or emphasis of a notion, and 2) complex formulas, such as kennings and merisms, that function as both symbolic and indexical signs.

Watkins explains that a "kenning is a bipartite figure of two nouns in a non-copulative, typically genitival grammatical relation (A of B) or in composition (B-A) which together make reference to, 'signify', a third notion C" (44). In other words, kennings are complex metaphoric phrases made of two concepts that together point to another concept which has a non-compositional meaning. For example, the genitive phrase "horse of the sea" translated from early Greek refers to a "ship," not to an equestrian creature in the ocean. Similarly, when Dickinson wrote of "silver fleeces" in the poem "A little East of Jordan" (Fr145), she was referring to "clouds," not to sheep's wool in the sky.

At the 2007 Emily Dickinson International Society conference, Rebecca Romney presented data and findings for a preliminary study of the role of kennings in Emily Dickinson's poems:

> Kenning, an Indo-European poetic formula that produces a compressed metaphor, is one type of circumlocution in Dickinson's poetry. The poems include two types of kenning structures: 1) genitive compounds

---

[18] Special thanks to my former research assistant Rachel (R'el) Johnston, who collaborated with me on the person name entries for the *Emily Dickinson Lexicon*.

and 2) non-genitive compounds. The genitive structures include the apostrophe formula *B's A = C*, as in "Morning's Nest" equals 'sunrise' (Fr346), and the prepositional formula *A of B = C*, as in "egg of forests" equals 'acorn' (Fr55). The non-genitive *B-A = C* structures include "Noun-Noun," as in "Alabaster Chambers" equals 'tombs' (Fr124); "Adjective-Noun," as in "silver fleeces" equals 'clouds' (Fr145); and "Verbal Adjective-Noun," as in "wheeling King" equals "the sun" (Fr246). Through kennings, Dickinson accesses specific qualities of a noun to create vibrant imagery.

Using the WordCruncher electronic concordance program, Romney found over 200 kennings in Dickinson's poems by searching for the preposition "of," the genitive inflection "'s," and noun adjunct compounds. Her analysis revealed that Dickinson employed kennings for euphemisms, riddles, and allusions.

For this essay, I used the search function of the *Emily Dickinson Lexicon* website (EDL) and found 75 kennings that had been included in definitions for headwords in Dickinson's poems. For each kenning, Table 1.6 provides its noun headward base and possible interpretations of the formula (see Appendix C). The EDL entry for the noun CONSENT shows how kennings can interplay with other language features for the same headword:

> Acceptance; approval; voluntary acquiescence; being in accord; having one heart and one mind; agreement with what another proposes or desires; [phrase "Consent of Language"] mutual understanding; loving communication through the philological power of words; [fig.] Logos; the Word; [metaphor] Jesus Christ (see John 1:1); condescension of God to offer His Son to save humans from physical and spiritual death (John 3:16); [kenning "Consent of Language"] charity; poetry more powerful than the "tongues of men and of angels" (1 Corinthians 13:1); pure and perfect communion through the love of God (see Zephaniah 3:9 "For then will I turn to the people a pure language, that they may call upon the name of the Lord, to serve him with one consent").

The word "consent" in Dickinson's poem "A word made Flesh" (Fr1715) is alive with multiple meanings that are as "Cohesive as the Spirit." In addition to the general denotations of the noun headword, the noun phrase "Consent of Language" has figurative, metaphorical, and indexical meanings, as well as biblical allusions of charity and future restorations of human language.

Metonymy in Emily Dickinson's Verse

Among the tools of living word-craft that Dickinson employed are traditional rhetorical figures such as metaphor and metonymy. In a psychological study of metaphor and metonymy in Dickinson's verse, Helene Knox explained that the poet combined the complementary and competitive capacity of both tropes in order to set boundaries metonymically and surpass them metaphorically in human and in alien dimensions. According to Stephen Ullman, while metaphor (and its sister term simile[19]) is a cognitive concept based on similarity of meaning, metonymy is a cognitive concept based on contiguity of meaning (cited in McMahon 182–183).

Dickinson's 1844 edition of Webster's dictionary allows us to view the terms metaphor and metonymy from a philological perspective. The ADEL entry for the noun METAPHOR provides a definition and a variety of examples:

> A short similitude; a similitude reduced to a single word; Or a word expressing similitude without the signs of comparison. Thus "that man is a fox," is a metaphor; but "that man is like a fox," is a similitude or comparison. So when I say, "the soldiers were lions in combat," I use a metaphor; but when I say, "the soldiers fought like lions," I use a similitude. In metaphor, the similitude is contained in the name; a man is a fox, means, a man is as crafty as a fox. So we say, a man bridles his anger, that is, restrains it as a bridle restrains a horse. Beauty awakens love or tender passions; opposition fires courage.[20]

In Dickinson's 1862 poem "There came a Day" (Fr325), the phrase "sealed church" can denote an ecclesiastical unit or a holy place, but metaphorically it can connote the symbolic corpus or body of Christ that worshippers partake of when they are "Permitted to commune" in the "Supper of the Lamb." On the other hand, as a metonym, the word "church" can mean that each of the individual participants can represent the whole congregation to one another, that the beloved alone is a sufficient community for the lover.

Metonymy yields poetic explanations of hierarchical relations, such as part-to-whole, cause-and-effect, species-genus, attribute-of-entity, hyponym-to-hypernym, producer-to-product, and so forth. The entry for the noun METONYMY in Webster's 1844 dictionary gives a definition and several examples of contiguous relationships:

---

[19] See http://edl.byu.edu/webster/term/2360751.
[20] See http://edl.byu.edu/webster/term/2377360.

> In rhetoric, a trope in which one word is put for another; a change of names which have some relation to each other; as when we say, "a man keeps a good table," instead of good provisions. "We read Virgil," that is, his poems or writings. "They have Moses and the prophets," that is, their books or writings. A man has a clear head, that is, understanding; intellect; a warm heart, that is, affections.[21]

Metonymy (and its sister term synecdoche)[22] gives life to Emily Dickinson's language by allowing one lexical item to refer to a contiguous item in the same semantic domain. Sometimes an instance of metonymy may use a whole to refer to a part, as in "Vision" referring to "eyes" in the 1862 poem "We grow accustomed to the Dark" (Fr428); however, more often instances of metonymy use a part to refer to the whole, as in "lips at Hallelujah" referring to a "choir" or "people singing" in the 1858 poem "The feet of people walking home" (Fr16). A word like "lips" can produce a polysemy of metonymy, referring to different meanings in various poems. For example, in the 1869 poem "I bring an unaccustomed wine" (Fr126), the word "lips" means a "person who is thirsty," whereas in the 1861 poem "Come slowly – Eden!" (Fr205), "Lips" are a metonymy for any "person" or "individual human being."

Table 1.7 provides a catalogue of metonymy occurrences that have been documented in entries for the *Emily Dickinson Lexicon* (see Appendix D). Notice that in many cases, the metonymic interpretation of a word can be accompanied by other figurative senses, including metaphors and kennings. For example, we can read the phrase "sites of Centres" as a metonym for "clusters of houses," but we can also read it as a kenning for the word "city" or "marketplace" (Fr1245). For Dickinson, language is a metonym of life, and each poem is a metonym of language. In each poem, a content word (noun, verb, or modifier) has the potential to represent either reality or immortality, the definite or the infinite, the particular or the eternal. Emily Dickinson incarnates each of her distinct words with a body and a spirit, with structure and meaning, with flesh and breath. Her language expires and inspires, feeds and intercedes. Each one of us has partaken of her life-giving sacramental language.

Love, Light, and the Breath of Life

In conclusion, when Dickinson wrote that her "business" was "to love" (L269), she may just have well said that her business was language. Philology, her love of language, led to her language of love, which carried light into the lives of those who received her verses. Like an artist, she saw the lines, shapes,

---

[21] See http://edl.byu.edu/webster/term/2377418.
[22] See http://edl.byu.edu/webster/term/2366136.

contours, and shadows of light in the play of human nature and divine creation. Instead of drawing or painting such details, she photographed in writings of light. She wrote in light, by light, of light, from light, and through light. For contrast, she also wrote of the dark, the shadows of doubt and death, but the secret of how her verses breathe is the pure love within her, and the source of her poetic power is the pure light around her.

In order to document the breath of life, the breadth of love, and the brightness of light in Dickinson's language, our scholarship should include philological criticism as one of the primary approaches to interpreting the poet's works. Emily Dickinson wrote that the "condescension" of Christ and the cohesive "consent" of language constitute a "loved Philology" (Fr1715). A philological criticism provides a way for readers to weave life, light, and love into textual interpretation. Philology gives life, breath, and spirit to language through the interacting etymology of people and words. Philology gives charity to our lives by teaching us the possibilities of language. A good reader posits that language is alive. Philological criticism allows language to breathe the spirit of life.

Etymology, the study of word histories, is an aspect of philology that documents the lexical-semantic life of language. Writers such as Emerson, Thoreau, and Dickinson made a conscious effort to build etymological associations into their works as a source of textual cohesion. Philological criticism does not foster "close reading" as the axe of structuralism or the hammer of formalism; rather, philology becomes a tool of tenderness. Dickinson's philology teaches us how to live, love, learn, and breathe in the house of Being.

The language of Emily Dickinson is sacramental, scriptural, traditional, and distinctive. The music of her language emulated the songs of nature and creation to which she had attuned her heart. The circumference of her language reverberated in microcosms and macrocosms of semantic, syntactic, thematic, and stylistic structures. Her collected poems comprise a body of living water, not a Dead Sea. She compiled and sealed up her book of *Revelation*, as if "such were for the Saints – / Where Resurrections – be –" (Fr325B).

Appendix A

Table 1.1 Catalogue of Emily Dickinson's Quoted Material

Franklin	Quotation Markings	Function	Source	Date
1605	'Come unto me'	literary	Matthew 11:28	1883
157	'Father, thy will be done'	literary	Matthew 6:10, Matthew 26:42	1860
139	'Houses'	literary	John 14:2	1860
139	'Mansions'	literary	John 14:2	1860
139	'Many Mansions' ... 'his Father'	literary	John 14:2	1860
48	'pleiad'	literary	star cluster myth	1859
165	'Volcanoes'	literary	*Atlantic Monthly* article	1860
372	'was it He, that bore'	dialogue, literary	Isaiah 53:12	1862
372	'Yesterday, or Centuries before'	dialogue		1862
384	"a fit"	figurative		1862
1540	"a fit."	emphasis		1880
933	"A Soul has gone to Heaven"	dialogue		1865
988	"A Thousand Times Thee Nay"	dialogue, literary	*Two Gentleman of Verona* 1.2.91	1865
101	"Action"	figurative	to reclaim her garden	1859
386	"Adam"	literary, name	Genesis 2:18-19	1862
1102	"admission"	humor		1865
1742	"Afraid he hissed / Of me"	dialogue		undated
1486	"Again"	self-quoting	quoting previous line of poem	1879
1297	"Alas"	dialogue		1873
1640	"all ... shall have their part in"	literary	Revelation 21:8	1884
1314	"All is possible with"	literary	Matthew 19:26	1874
1370	"All"	emphasis		1875

274	"alone"	emphasis		1862
241	"Amherst"	name	Dickinson's hometown	1861
448	"And I – for Truth – Themself are One – / We Bretheren, are"	dialogue, literary	allusion to Keats's "Ode on a Grecian Urn"	1862
1177	"and not you."	emphasis		1870
346	"And now, Would'st have me for a Guest"	dialogue, literary	Revelation 3:20	1862
1537	"And with what Body do they come"	literary	1 Corinthians 15:35	1880
828	"And yet Thou art industrious – / No need – had'st Thou – of us –"	dialogue		1864
117	"Arcturus"	name	star in Ursa Major; brightest star in the Big Dipper constellation	1859
825	"Arms of Mine – sufficient Phaeton – / Trust Omnipotence"	dialogue		1864
812	"As large as I"	dialogue		1864
155	"Augustan"	humor, literary	wordplay on Caesar Augustus	1860
465	"Autumn"	emphasis		1862
229	"Band"	emphasis		1861
175	"Beam"	literary	possibly J. G. Whittier's "Snowbound"	1860
244	"beat; Wife"	humor, emphasis		1861
1577	"believe"	literary	Mark 9:23	1882
1021	"Bird within the Hand"	literary	proverb	1865
1236	"bit of noise"	dialogue		1871
239	"bloom"	humor, emphasis	same as above	1861

Dickinson's Breath of Life

1537	"Body"	literary	1 Corinthians 15:35	1880
2	"Bonnie Doon"	name	"Bonnie Dundee" = Bobbie Burns	1852
798	"Branch", and "Jugular"	literary	possibly from a botany textbook, like Cutter's 1852 *Treatise on Anatomy, Physiology, and Hygiene*	1864
496	"Bread –"	dialogue		1862
1266	"Breadth"	emphasis, dialogue	quoting preacher from poem	1872
1021	"Bush"	literary	proverb	1865
687	"But – Madam – is there nothing else – / That we can show – Today"	dialogue		1863
87	"But I have chosen them"	literary	John 15:16	1859
1056	"But just to be a Bee"	dialogue, literary	Isaac Watts	1865
117	"Cabinets"	humor		1859
179	"Canaan"	literary	Deuteronomy 32:48-49	1860
117	"Centipede"	humor		1859
164	"Charming April Day"	dialogue		1860
117	"Children"	literary	Matthew 18:3	1859
117	"Class"	humor		1859
179	"Classify"	humor		1860
1766	"Come home with me, my friend; / My parlor is of shriven glass, / My pantry has a fish / For every palate in the Year,"	dialogue		undated

1623	"Come in"	dialogue		1883
1617	"Come unto me"	literary	Matthew 11:28	1883
43	"Come"	dialogue		1858
1275	"Come"	dialogue		1872
147	"Comparative Anatomy"	literary	Alexander Monro, 1744; William Lawrence, 1861; Richard Owen, 1843	1860
1640	"Conscience"	figurative, name		1884
434	"Conscious"	dialogue		1862
252	"consider"	literary	Luke 6:28, 12:24	1861
128	"Crown"	literary	2 Timothy 4:8; James 1:12; or Revelation 2:10	1859
1386	"Crowns of Life"	literary	Revelation 2:11	1876
146	"Currer Bell"	name	Charlotte Bronte's pen name	1860
148	"Day"	emphasis		1860
239	"Day"	dialogue		1861
277	"Day"	dialogue		1862
384	"Dead"	dialogue		1862
384	"Dead"	dialogue		1862
550	"Despair"	emphasis		1863
105	"Death"	emphasis		1859
249	"Death"	figurative		1861
328	"Defeat"	emphasis		1862
147	"Departed"	dialogue		1860
1640	"Did you; Did you not,"	dialogue		1884
943	"Did'st thou; Thou did'st not mean"	dialogue		1865
241	"die"	emphasis		1861
249	"difficult the gate"	literary	Matthew 7:15	1861

1768	"Disciple, call again."	dialogue		undated
249	"Discount"	figurative		1861
153	"dishonor"	literary	1 Corinthians 15:42-43	1860
973	"Dissolve"	dialogue		1865
121	"Diver."	literary	Malay pearl divers; *Atlantic Monthly* article	1859
249	"Dividend"	figurative		1861
207	"drams"	figurative		1861
96	"Duke of Exeter"	literary, name	Shakespeare's *Henry V* 3.6.5-16	1859
119	"dying"	emphasis		1859
265	"Dying"	emphasis		1861
62	"Early dead"	emphasis, literary	*The Early Dead; Or, Our Loved and Lost Ones. A Selection of Poetry*, 1853	1859
166	"Early history"	humor		1860
482	"Easy ... to die"	dialogue		1862
241	"Eden"	literary	Revelation 21:18	1861
301	"Elder"	emphasis		1862
198	"Emily"	name	the poet Emily Dickinson herself	1861
249	"enter in – thereat"	literary	Matthew 7:17	1861
144	"Escape"	emphasis		1860
1261	"Eye hath not seen"	literary	1 Corinthians 2:9	1872
119	"fade"	self-quoting	refers to previous line of poem	1859
119	"fading"	emphasis		1859
202	"Faith"	emphasis		1861
1386	"Faithful to the end"	literary	Revelation 2:10	1876
241	"Farmers"	emphasis		1861

241	"Father"	emphasis		1861
849	"Fellow / Of the Royal"	emphasis		1864
249	"few there be"	literary	Matthew 7:16	1861
1552	"Few"	emphasis		1881
179	"flowers"	emphasis		1860
1253	"foolish Tun"	dialogue		1872
448	"For Beauty"	dialogue		1862
198	"Forbid us not"	literary	Matthew 19:14	1861
252	"forgiven"	emphasis		1861
252	"forgiven"	emphasis		1861
42	"forgot"	emphasis		1858
244	"Found dead; of Nectar"	humor, emphasis		1861
482	"General, the British"	dialogue		1862
244	"get drunk"	humor, emphasis		1861
494	"Get out of the Way, I say"	dialogue		1862
581	"Give Me"	dialogue		1863
988	"Give of thine an Acre unto me"	dialogue		1865
1584	"Go tell it"	literary	Spartan warriors' epitaph at Thermopylae, mentioned by Simonedes and Herodotus	1882
249	"go to Jail"	figurative		1861
1561	"Go traveling with us"	dialogue		1881
432	"God have mercy"	dialogue		1862
1314	"God is Love"	literary	1 John 4:8	1874
1277	"God took him"	literary	Genesis 5:24	1873
292	"God"	dialogue		1862

910	"Golden Fleece"	literary	Myth – Jason and the argonauts	1865
123	"Golden Rod"	literary	William Cullen Bryant, "but on the hills of goldenrod"	1859
1328	"Good Morning"	dialogue		1874
97	"Good night"	dialogue		1859
127	"Good night"	dialogue		1859
736	"Great"	self-quoting	quoting previous line of poem	1863
776	"Hamlet"	literary	Shakespeare's play	1863
434	"Happy"	dialogue		1862
1304	"Have altered – Accept the pillage / for the progress' sake"	dialogue		1873
146	"Haworth"	name	Brontes' hometown	1860
582	"Hay"	emphasis		1863
167	"Heart's Ease"	name	Viola tricolor; "Johnny Jump-up" pansy	1860
117	"Heaven"	humor		1859
309	"Heaven"	emphasis		1862
544	"Heaven"	emphasis		1863
1500	"Heavenly Father"	literary	Matthew 6:14	1879
1564	"Here; Heres"	self-quoting	quoting previous line	1881
405	"Hide and Seek"	name	a children's game	1862
2	"Hill of Science"	literary	Webster; phrase appears in his primer	1852
166	"his Father"	humor		1860
241	"hoe"	emphasis		1861

434	"Homesick"	dialogue		1862
314	"Hope"	emphasis		1862
12	"house at hame"	literary	Bobbie Burns's poetry	1858
1333	"How are you"	dialogue		1874
605	"How cold – it grew"	dialogue		1863
2	"How doth the busy bee"	literary	Isaac Watts	1852
1742	"How fair you are"	dialogue		undated
429	"How shall you know"	dialogue		1862
391	"How to forget"	self-quoting	quoting line 1	1862
1372	"How trivial is Life"	dialogue		1875
1372	"How vast a Destiny"	dialogue		1875
217	"how"	dialogue		1861
1015	"I am great and cannot wait / So therefore let me in"	dialogue		1865
1275	"I am he / You cherished"	dialogue		1872
825	"I am Jesus – Late of Judea – / Now – of Paradise"	dialogue		1864
1342	"I am not consumed ... / Yet saw him face to face"	literary	Exodus 3:2, Exodus 33:11	1874
825	"I am Pardon"	dialogue		1864
725	"I dont know"	dialogue		1863
708	"I see Thee"	dialogue		1863
266	"I vow to pay / To Her – who pledges this – / One hour – of her Sovreign's face"	literary	Shakespeare, *Richard the Second* 2.1.170	1861
851	"I want"	dialogue		1864
145	"I will not let thee go / Except thou bless me"	literary	Genesis 32:26	1860

1786	"if I could"	dialogue		undated
575	"If I should be a Queen, Tomorrow"	dialogue		1863
317	"If it would last"	dialogue		1862
1566	"If you dare"	dialogue		1881
1013	"I'll meet You"	dialogue		1865
429	"I'm Midnight"	dialogue		1862
429	"I'm Sunrise"	dialogue		1862
41	"it's I"	dialogue		1858
241	"Jasper"	literary	Revelation 21:18	1861
1314	"jealous god"	literary	Exodus 20:5	1874
222	"Jesus"	name, literary	Matthew 1:1	1861
366	"John"	literary	John 19:26	1862
437	"Judgement Day"	emphasis		1862
266	"June"	emphasis		1861
478	"Just Once"	dialogue, self-quoting	quoting line 1	1862
1784	"keeping house"	figurative		undated
38	"Kidd"	name	Captain Kidd; Stevenson's *Treasure Island*	1858
117	"kingdom of Heaven's"	literary	Matthew 5:3	1859
207	"Landlords"	figurative		1861
178	"Laureates"	literary, figurative	Park & Sharpe's *Works of the British Poets*, pp. 72-73	1860
1275	"Learned Waters – / Wisdom is stale – to Me"	dialogue		1872
1275	"Let me grow"	dialogue		1872
54	"Lethe"	literary	Myth/Dante = river of forgetfulness	1859
1314	"Life that is to be,"	emphasis		1874

1314	"Life that is"	emphasis		1874
849	"Line"	emphasis		1864
232	"looked"	literary	Luke 22:54-65	1861
363	"Lost"	emphasis		1862
1577	"lost"	literary	John 17:12	1882
130	"Mama"	name	common usage; diminutive of 'Mother'	1859
151	"Mansion"	literary	John 14:2	1860
375	"Me – Miss – me"	dialogue		1862
255	"Me"	dialogue		1861
2	"memento mori"	literary	Plato	1852
324	"Memnon"	name	Egyptian ruler	1862
615	"Miles; John Alden"	literary	Henry Wadsworth Longfellow's "The Courtship of Miles Standish"	1863
615	"Miles; Priscilla"	literary, names	Henry Wadsworth Longfellow's "The Courtship of Miles Standish"	1863
191	"Milking"	emphasis		1861
268	"minor"	emphasis		1861
229	"Morning Stars"	literary	Job 38:4-7	1861
148	"morning"	emphasis		1860
148	"morning"	emphasis		1860
191	"Morning"	emphasis		1861
191	"Morning"	emphasis		1861
179	"Moses"	literary, name	Exodus 2:10	1860
440	"My Business but a Life I left / Was such remaining there?"	dialogue		1862

1015	"My Faces are asleep / But swear, and I will let you by / You will not wake them up"	dialogue		1865
194	"My Husband"	dialogue		1861
393	"Myself"	emphasis		1862
166	"native town."	humor		1860
721	"Nature"	emphasis	lines 1, 5, and 9	1863
350	"Nay"	dialogue		1862
117	"new fashioned"	humor		1859
229	"New Life"	literary	Romans 6:4	1861
241	"new shoes; Eden"	emphasis, literary	Ezekiel 28:13	1861
1742	"No Cordiality"	dialogue		undated
402	"No Sir! In Thee!"	dialogue		1862
232	"No"	literary	Luke 22:54-64	1861
346	"No"	dialogue		1862
235	"not at home"	dialogue	phrase taught to footman	1861
894	"Not at Home"	dialogue		1865
346	"Not so"	dialogue		1862
1611	"Nothing"	self-quoting	quoting previous line	1883
234	"noticed"	emphasis		1861
1056	"off the Bar"	literary?	possibly Norie's 1818 *New and Complete Sailing Directions for the East Coasts of England and Scotland*	1865
114	"Oh could we climb where Moses stood, / And view the Landscape o'er"	literary	paraphrase of lines in Isaac Watts's hymn "There is a land of pure delight"	1859

117	"Oh Lord, how frail are we"	literary	hymn 647 in *An Arrangement of the Psalms, Hymns and Spiritual Songs*, 1801	1859
117	"Old fashioned"	humor		1859
996	"Old Friend, thou knowest Me"	dialogue, literary	Jeremiah 12:1	1865
1271	"Ought to"	humor, dialogue		1872
134	"Paradise"	literary	Luke 23:43	1859
241	"Paradise"	emphasis		1861
117	"pearl"	literary	Revelation 21:21, pearly gates	1859
145	"Peniel"	literary	Genesis 32:30	1860
1177	"Peradventure"	dialogue		1870
164	"Peter Parley"	name	pseudonym of publisher Samuel Griswold Goodrich	1860
215	"Peter"	literary	Matthew 26:33-35	1861
849	"Pine"	emphasis		1864
851	"Please"	dialogue		1864
923	"Please"	dialogue		1865
12	"Pleiad"	literary	star cluster myth	1858
168	"Pompeii"	literary	*Atlantic Monthly* article	1860
394	"Poor Child"	dialogue		1862
118	"Potosi"	name	Potosi, Bolivia, famous for its silver mines; the largest silver deposit ever found	1859
525	"pray"	emphasis		1863
169	"Preferment"	emphasis		1860

615	"Priscilla"	literary	Henry Wadsworth Longfellow's "The Courtship of Miles Standish"	1863
136	"Promoted"	emphasis		1860
208	"Recess"	humor		1861
1681	"Red Sea,"	literary	Exodus 15:4	1885
1208	"Remember Me"	literary	Luke 23:42	1871
425	"Reprieve"	dialogue		1862
117	"Resurgam"	humor		1859
137	"Resurrection"	figurative, literary	John 11:24-25	1860
500	"Revelation"	emphasis, literary	Bible: The Revelation of St John the Divine	1863
179	"Revelations"	literary	Bible: The Revelation of St John the Divine	1860
394	"Rich People"	humor		1862
455	"Rich"	dialogue		1862
179	"Right hand"	literary	1 Kings 22:19; Matthew 25:33	1860
128	"Robe"	literary	Revelation 6:11, 7:13-15	1859
776	"Romeo"	literary	character in Shakespeare's play *Romeo and Juliet*	1863
117	"Savan"	humor		1859
175	"Scaffold"	literary	possibly J. G. Whittier's "Snowbound"	1860

1494	"Secrets"	emphasis		1879
1130	"Secure your Flower"	dialogue		1866
266	"share; Banks"	figurative, humor	figurative wordplay	1861
101	"Shaw"	name	Henry Shaw; day laborer who would dig for Dickinson's garden	1859
123	"sheaves"	literary	James Thomson (1700-1748) "Crown'd with the sickle, and the wheaten sheaf"; or John O. Thompson (1782-1818); or James Oren Thompson (1834-1917), "Send them now the sheaves to gather" and "Gather now the sheaves of gold."	1859
266	"Shylock"	literary	Shakespeare, *The Merchant of Venice*	1861
973	"Sir / I have another Trust"	dialogue		1865
239	"skim"	humor, emphasis	flowers should bloom, and butterflies skim, not the reverse	1861
56	"skirmish"	figurative		1859
119	"sleep"	emphasis		1859
307	"small"	dialogue, self-quoting	quoting lines 13 and 14 of poem	1862
307	"small"	emphasis		1862
541	"so loved"	literary	John 3:16	1863
394	"sorry I am dead"	dialogue		1862

153	"Sown in corruption"	literary	1 Corinthians 15:42-43	1860
153	"Sown in dishonor"	literary	1 Corinthians 15:42-43	1860
252	"sparrow"	literary	Luke 12:6	1861
130	"sparrows fall"	literary	Matthew 10:29	1859
410	"spicy isles –"	literary	Darwin collaborator Alfred Russell Wallace explored the Spice Islands in 1862	1862
265	"Spring"	emphasis		1861
602	"St James"	name	English royal court, a residence of the British monarch	1863
117	"Star"	emphasis		1859
169	"Station"	emphasis		1860
445	"still"	emphasis, dialogue	as in "hold still"	1862
266	"stocks"	figurative		1861
265	"Summer"	emphasis		1861
1316	"Sunset"	emphasis		1874
325	"Supper of the Lamb"	literary	Revelation 19:9	1862
328	"Surrender"	emphasis		1862
496	"Sweet Lady – Charity"	dialogue	Catholic prayer to Mary	1862
482	"Sweet ... my own Surrender / Liberty's beguile"	dialogue	textbook for story, if not exact quotes?	1862
357	"Take Courage, Friend – / That – was a former time – / But we might learn to like the Heaven, / As well as our Old Home"	dialogue		1862
41	"take Dollie"	dialogue	pet name for Sue	1858

1110	"Thanksgiving Day"	emphasis	lines 2, 16	1865
204	"That must have seen the Sun"	dialogue		1861
1280	"the Father and the Son"	literary	1 John 2:22, 2 John 1:9	1873
1391	"The House not made with Hands"	literary	2 Corinthians 5:1	1876
825	"The Least / Is esteemed in Heaven the Chiefest – / Occupy my House"	dialogue, literary	Matthew 18:4; Mark 10:44; John 14:2	1864
169	"the Lord of Lords"	literary	Deuteronomy 10:14; Psalms 136:3; Revelation 17:14	1860
834	"The Other – She – is Where"	dialogue		1864
229	"the Spheres"	literary	Pythagoras	1861
1540	"the stars;"	emphasis		1880
249	"the way is narrow"	literary	Matthew 7:14	1861
117	"the worst"	literary	Ezekiel 7:24	1859
1275	"then you will be a Sea – / I want a brook – Come now"	dialogue		1872
30	"*There* is no more snow"	dialogue		1858
708	"These see"	emphasis		1863
602	"they are dying mostly – now"	dialogue		1863
87	"They have not chosen me"	literary	John 15:16	1859
695	"thirst no more"	literary	John 4:13	1863
621	"This was last Her fingers did"	dialogue		1863
575	"This was she – / Begged in the Market place – Yesterday."	dialogue, literary	John 9:8	1863
1594	"this way"	dialogue		1882

267	"Thorns"	literary	John 19:2, Crown of thorns	1861
828	"Thou hast not Me, nor Me"	dialogue		1864
1768	"Thou shalt not"	literary	Exodus 20:3-17	undated
232	"Thou wert with him; the Damsel"	literary	Luke 22:54-63	1861
231	"Tim"	name, literary	Tiny Tim in Dickens	1861
861	"Time assuages"	dialogue		1864
1574	"to come"	emphasis	Matthew 12:32; Mark 10:30; Luke 18:30	1882
619	"To die"	emphasis		1863
189	"Toby"	name	the Dickinson family cat	1861
1417	"Tomorrow"	self-quoting	quoting her own letter's announcement that "Austin will come tomorrow" (L490)	1877
1031	"Trotwood"	literary	character in Dickens's novel *David Copperfield*	1865
1266	"Truth"	emphasis		1872
402	"Tune is in the Tree"	dialogue		1862
1775	"'Twas all I had,"	dialogue		undated
730	"'Twas only a Balloon"	dialogue		1863
589	"'Twas Sunset"	dialogue		1863
261	"'Twill keep"	dialogue		1861
1304	"Unchanged"	dialogue		1873
814	"Undiscovered Continent"	emphasis	possibly Helps's 1869 *The Life of Columbus: The Discoverer of America*	1864

825	"Unto Me"	literary	Matthew 11:28	1864
126	"Unto the little, unto me"	literary	Bible paraphrase: Matthew 25:40	1859
274	"vailed faces"	literary	Exodus 34:33	1862
2	"view the Landscape o're"	literary	Isaac Watts	1852
232	"Warmed them; Temple fire"	literary	Luke 22:54-62	1861
719	"Was buried; Buried; He!"	dialogue, literary	1 Corinthians 15:4	1863
736	"was Great"	dialogue		1863
605	"Was it conscious – when it stepped / In Immortality"	dialogue		1863
1277	"Was Not"	literary	Genesis 5:24	1873
1500	"We are Dust"	literary	Psalms 103:14	1873
1328	"We dreamed it"	dialogue		1874
384	"When tomorrow comes this way – / I shall have waded down one Day"	dialogue		1862
311	"Where"	dialogue		1862
1013	"Where"	dialogue		1865
823	"Which choose I"	dialogue		1864
823	"Which choose They"	dialogue		1864
482	"Which obtain the Day"	dialogue		1862
401	"White Heat"	literary	Spurgeon's *Sermons*, volume 15: 1869, p. 435	1862
268	"White Robe"	literary	Revelation 6:11, white robes given to martyrs, including St. Peter	1861

711	"Whoever Ye shall ask – / Itself be given You"	literary	Matthew 21:22	1863
311	"Who's there"	dialogue		1862
459	"Why do I love"	dialogue		1862
448	"Why I failed"	dialogue		1862
217	"Why"	dialogue		1861
1392	"why"	dialogue		1876
225	"wife"	emphasis		1861
225	"Wife"	emphasis		1861
267	"Wife's"	emphasis		1861
346	"With me"	dialogue		1862
225	"Woman"	emphasis		1861
712	"Would I be Whole"	dialogue		1863
346	"Would'st Climb"	dialogue		1862
668	"Ye Blessed"	literary	Matthew 25:34	1863
346	"Yes"	dialogue		1862
556	"You know me – Sir"	dialogue		1863
1304	"you"	dialogue		1873
181	"you're hurt"	dialogue		1860
1015	"You're soon"	dialogue		1865
117	"Zenith"	humor		1859
157	"Victory"	dialogue		1860

Appendix B

Table 1.2 Sample of Emily Dickinson's Language Features

Language Features	Linguistic Category	Definition	Example	Franklin
ALLITERATION	Sound Repetition & Variation	repetition of initial sounds	/b/; breath blew back	132
ALLUSION	Pragmatics	cross-textual reference to a prior text, usually one well known by others	the first was the last … the last was the first (Matthew 19:30)	1753
ANACOLUTHON	Syntax	garden-path structure; syntactic doubling; digression of syntactic structure so that a sentence begins with a clause that is never resolved and ends with a different clause	And was about to ring / for the suspended Candidate / There came unsummoned in	1243
ANADIPLOSIS	Word Repetition & Variation	the final word(s) of one phrase or clause are the initial word(s) of the next	When the Ball enters, enters Silence	616
ANAPHORA	Word Repetition & Variation	repetition of initial words or phrases in successive language units	It sifts … It powders … It fills … It traverses	291
ANTIMETABOLE	Word Repetition & Variation	words repeated in inverse order, often in an A-B-B-A pattern	Reality a Dream / And Dreams, Reality	1633
ANTIMETABOLIC SEQUENCE	Sound Repetition & Variation	repetition of sounds in inverse order	/f, s, s, f/; Fast in a safer hand	4

ANTITHESIS	Semantics and Lexis	words or phrases that contrast in meaning	The Opening and the Close / Of Being	1089
ASSONANCE	Sound Repetition & Variation	repetition of vowel sounds	/i, i, i, i/; Eternity will be / Velocity	1354
ASYNDETON	Syntax	deletion of conjunctions between words in a series	the Whole of Love, The Alphabet, the Words, A Chapter, the mighty Book	531
AUXESIS	Semantics and Lexis	a series of words or ideas that increase (or decrease) in length, size, or degree within a passage	Bees > Butterflies > Swans > Giants – practicing / Titanic Opera	627
BREVIA	Style	succinctness; a terse style with concise expressions	Fame is a bee.	1788
CATALOGUE	Semantics and Lexis	a long list of elements in a series	I like to see it lap ... lick ... stop ... step ... peer ... pare ... crawl ... chase ... neigh ... Then – prompter than a Star / Stop	383
CHIASMUS	Semantics and Lexis	similar word meanings or repeated phrases in inverse order, often framing a central point	I shall know why ... I have ceased to wonder ... Christ will explain ... He will tell me ... And I – for wonder ... I shall forget ...	215

CONSONANCE	Sound Repetition & Variation	repetition of consonant sounds	/t, p, t, r, pr, t/; what "Peter" promised	215
DEFINITION	Semantics and Lexis	a statement of the meaning(s) of a term	Shame is the shawl of Pink / In which we wrap the Soul	1437
ELLIPSIS	Syntax	omission of part of a phrase or clause structure that can be understood from contiguity of form or grammatical context	Nor then perhaps [is] reported	1715
EPANADIPLOSIS	Word Repetition & Variation	repetition of the word(s) at the beginning and end of one phrase or clause	Brain of his Brain	264
EPANALEPSIS	Word Repetition & Variation	general repetition of words, not specifically or exclusively at the beginning or end of language units	Day, Day, Day	1372
EPISTROPHE	Word Repetition & Variation	repetition of final words	Tim and I	231
EPIZEUXIS	Word Repetition & Variation	immediate repetition of adjacent words	'Tis so much joy! 'Tis so much joy!	170
FULL RHYME	Sound Repetition & Variation	exact repetition of final nucleus vowel + coda consonant sounds in words at the end of successive or alternating phrases/clauses	/er, er/ and /aif, aif/; everywhere … crowded air … silver strife … 'New Life'!	229

HENDIADYS	Semantics and Lexis	an idea expressed by two nouns connected by "and" instead of being expressed by a noun and a qualifier; any expression in which coordinate words are used when one word would have been subordinated to modify the other	The Lingering – and the Stain = 'the long-lasting color'	549
HOMOEOTELEUTON	Sound Repetition & Variation	repetition of final consonant sounds; sometimes called NEAR RHYME	/l/; well, still, full	823
HYPERBATON	Syntax	unusual inversion of standard word order	He keeps His Secrets safely – very	677
IDENTICAL RHYME	Sound Repetition & Variation	rhyming of the same word or part of a word	Drop a Tune on Me ... What will become of Me?	915
INTERNAL RHYME	Sound Repetition & Variation	repetition of final sounds in words within a phrase or clause	anterior, posterior	980
INVERSION	Syntax	variation on standard word order as a poetic convention	Some things that fly there be	68
IRONY	Pragmatics	an expression that highlights an unexpected turn in meaning or unusual juxtaposition of elements	Sparrows, unnoticed by the Father; see Matthew 10:29-31	91

ISOCOLON	Syntax	successive phrases or clauses with the same number of syllables	3 syllables + 3 syllables: Out of sound – out of sight	534
KENNING	Syntax	metaphoric pair, showing a relation of similarity, often genitive or compound in form	Awful Father of Love = God	1200
LITOTES	Semantics and Lexis	an affirmative concept stated in a negated form; definition by stating what something is not; for example, "not bad" = "good"	undelaying = endless, constant, reliable	1106
MERISM	Syntax	metonymic pair, showing a relation of contiguity, where two hyponyms represent a larger class	Brooch and Earrings = jewelry = poetry	553
METAPHOR	Semantics and Lexis	juxtaposition and/or identification of two concepts with similar meanings	Volcano = those old – phlegmatic mountains	165
NEOLOGISM	Semantics and Lexis	a new word "coined" into the language or borrowed from another language	An Optizan / Could not decide between	608
OXYMORON	Semantics and Lexis	the juxtaposition of paradoxical or contradicting ideas	'Twas a Divine Insanity	593

PAIRS	Syntax	sets of two synonymous, complementary, or antithetical words	a spectre's cloak / Hid Heaven and Earth from view	224
PARALLELISM	Semantics and Lexis	successive phrases or clauses with similar meanings	I cannot buy it – 'tis not sold –	943
PARENTHESIS	Syntax	a phrase or clause that interrupts an idea	A few – and they by Risk – procure	560
PARISON	Syntax	successive phrases or clauses with the same syntactic structures	White as an Indian Pipe / Red as a Cardinal Flower	1193
PARODY	Pragmatics	imitation of themes and formulas in a prior text	In the name of the Bee ... the Butterfly ... the Breeze	23
PAROMOION	Sound Repetition & Variation	repetition of initial and final sounds between two different words; a combination of alliteration and homoeoteleuton	/m...n, m...n/; A Mine there is no Man would own	1162
PERIPHRASIS	Semantics and Lexis	circumlocution; circuit; a long or roundabout way of expressing the meaning of a word, a phrase, or an idea	identity = The face I carry with me	395
PLEONASM	Semantics and Lexis	redundancy; synonymy; repetition of synonymous words or phrases	This is the Sovereign Anguish! / This – the signal woe!	178

POLYPTOTON	Word Repetition & Variation	repetition or variation of words with the same morphological root or base	Reverse ... Adversity	565
POLYSEMY	Semantics and Lexis	use of multiple meanings of a word	"Augustan" = 'eighth month' and 'pertaining to Caesar' and 'stately, majestic'	155
POLYSYNDETON	Syntax	words or phrases joined by conjunctions in a series	There's Sarah, and Eliza, and Emmeline so fair, / And Harriet, and Susan, and she with curling hair!	1
PUN	Semantics and Lexis	paronomasia; homonymic wordplay created by two words that sound the same but have different meanings	As if no soul the solstice passed	325
REGISTER	Style	levels of formality in speech and writing, such as frozen, high, normal, low, colloquial, and so forth	high register: Shall I take thee, the Poet said / To the propounded word?	1243
RIDDLE	Pragmatics	a lyric formula that requires a reader to guess what the author is describing	Barbs it has, like a Bee!	71
RING COMPOSITION	Word Repetition & Variation	a text that begins and ends with the same word(s)	Soul ... Soul!	89

SENSE PLAY	Semantics and Lexis	polysemy; wordplay created by using two different senses of one word	minor = small / music key; Mass = church service / group of creatures	895
SONANCE	Sound Repetition & Variation	rich combination of various sound figures	/fst, n, s,f,r hænd, h,ld, n, tr,r, lænd/; Fast in a safer hand / Held in a truer Land	4
SORIASMUS	Semantics and Lexis	combination of words derived from different languages, especially words contrasting between Germanic and Latinate vocabulary in English	A full, and perfect time; Germanic 'full' + Latinate 'perfect', conjoined pair	822
SOUND PLAY	Sound Repetition & Variation	juxtaposition of two different words with similar sounds in close proximity	/mis/ and /miz/; I know lives, I could miss / Without a Misery	574
STEM VOWEL CHANGE	Morphology and Grammar	use of an umlaut vowel substitution to indicate a grammatical function, such as past tense or plural	Glid (instead of the regular past tense 'glided')	43
SYMPLOCE	Word Repetition & Variation	repetition of the same initial and final words in successive phrases or clauses	If I can ... I shall not live in vain / If I can ... I shall not live in Vain	982
TRIADS	Syntax	sets of three synonymous or complementary words	Neighbor – and friend – and Bridegroom	685

WORD CHAIN	Semantics and Lexis	a set of words or images from the same semantic domain, which seem to tie a text together	dwell, House, Windows, Doors, Chambers, Roof, Gambrels	466
WORDPLAY	Semantics and Lexis	creation of a new meaning by applying word roots to other semantic domains	Logarithm – had I – for Drink; logarithym = logos + rhythm = word + meter = 'poetry'	754

Appendix C

Table 1.6 Sample of Emily Dickinson's Kennings

Headword	Franklin	Kenning	Interpretation Comments
auctioneer, n.	1646	Auctioneer of Parting	death
Bethlehem, proper n.	251	Star of Bethlehem	Christ; beloved Son of God; Deity of the New Testament
bisecting, verbal adj.	1421	Bisecting Messenger	angel of Death; harbinger of passing from mortality to immortality
board, n.	475	Art of Boards	carpentry; construction; architecture; skill with woodworking
camel, n.	770	Camel's trait	abstinence; temperance
casement, n.	65	floating casement	Noah's ark (see Genesis 8)
cash, n.	526	Satin Cash	unconventional currency made of flower petals
cedar, adj.	1536	Cedar Floor	forest; grove of evergreen trees
celestial, adj.	1380	celestial Mail	endowment; investiture; atonement; holy ordinance; temple covenant
chosen, verbal adj.	1032	Chosen Child	Christ; Anointed One (see Luke 23:35)
chronicle, n.	810	Silver Chronicle	birdsong
claw, n.	1032	Claw of Dragon	danger; death; evil
Cleopatra, proper n.	696	Cleopatra's Company	resplendent; golden sunset; display
consent, n.	1715	consent of Language	charity; poetry more powerful than the "tongues of men and of angels" (see 1 Corinthians 13:1); pure and perfect communion through the love of God (see Zephaniah 3:9 "For then will I turn to the people a pure language, that they may call upon the name of the Lord, to serve him with one consent")
country, adj.	547	Country Town	village; settlement

crown, n.	1386	Crowns of Life	heavenly reward; divine recompense; compensation for those who overcome trials; honor for saints who endure persecution (see James 1:12; Revelation 2:10)
day, n.	970	Days is He	progenitor
death, n.	1769	House of Death	tomb; grave; sepulchre
debauchee, n.	140	Debauchee of Dews	bee; flying insect that collects pollen to make honey
debauchee, n.	207	Debauchee of Dew	hummingbird
delight, n.	1147	Republic of Delight	Eden; paradise
delight, n.	1406	Delights of Dust	lifetime
door, n.	1401	Purple Door	dream world
earthen, adj.	845	Earthen Door	horizon; skyline
emerald, adj.	1618	Emerald Ghost	tornado; tempest; twisting cloud
eternal, adj.	646	Eternal Rule	Deity; God; the Supreme Being; the King of Heaven
ethereal, adj.	794	Ethereal Zone	immortality; paradise; Elysium; spirit world; place beyond the veil of death
fleece, n.	141	silver fleece	moonlight; reflected light of the moon from the invisible sun
flesh, adj.	305	fleshly Gate	mortality; physical body; bondage of earthly life
flower, n.	141	Couch of flowers	field; garden
forest, n.	171	Forest Folk	birds or insects
garnet, adj.	1161	Garnet Tooth	fiery volcanic eruption; glowing stream of lava
hill, n.	162	Wood and Hill	forest
hoof, n.	1506	Hoofs of the Clock	minutes; quick-paced temporal units
identity, n.	1731	mansion of Identity	divinity; godliness; unique intelligence; spiritual reality
immortal, adj.	122	immortal wine	nectar; drink that enables one to live forever
king, n.	1352	King of Down	comforter

Dickinson's Breath of Life 49

kinsman, n.	512	Kinsmen of the Shelf	books; authors; story characters
lap, n.	363	lap of Adamant	snowbank; frozen garden
let, n.	254	Let of Snow	snowfall
life, n.	259	Dial life	mortality; earth life
lip, n.	210	Granite lip	cold corpse; dead body
liquid, adj.	730	Liquid Feet	ropes; cords; strings; mooring cables
lone, adj.	1149	lone Orthography	epitaph; individual gravestone inscription in a cemetery or an abandoned battlefield
low, adj.	698	the lower Way	mortality
maple, adj.	915	Maple Keep	nest
merchant, n.	1134	Merchant of the Picturesque	Creator; Divine Redeemer
moat, n.	134	moat of pearl	pearly gate (see Revelation 21:21)
moat, n.	1644	Moats of Mystery	cloud banks that veil the view of heaven
moccasin, n.	1618	Electric Moccasin	lightning strike
mold, n.	93	memorial mold	death
mystery, n.	90	Nicodemus' Mystery	baptism and resurrection = spring
orthography, n.	1149	lone Orthography	personal epitaph; individual gravestone inscription
place, n.	901	Sheets of Place	fields; farms; homesteads
sapphire, adj.	589	Sapphire Farm	universe; solar system; galaxy; Milky Way
sea, n.	571	Ether Sea	the sky
sentinel, n.	912	Nature's sentinels	creatures; birds
seventy, adj.	1483	Seventy Years	a lifetime; a human being's average life span
shawl, n.	1437	shawl of Pink	blush; flush of circulating blood; reddish coloring of the skin due to embarrassment
shore, n.	136	Pizarro's shore	paradise; new world
silver, adj.	145	silver fleeces	white clouds

silver, adj.	229	silver strife	melodious birdsong
silver, adj.	131	silver apron	filigreed foliage
silver, adj.	950	Silver Fracture	ice; frost; sheet of shining crystallized frozen water
silver, adj.	513	Silver Ball	sticky white substance for building delicate webs
sky, n.	437	Handsome Skies	heavenly domain; celestial kingdom
sod, n.	286	Sod Gown	western horizon
solid, adj.	656	Solid Town	shore; land above a beach
summer, n.	13	summer's brows	crops; harvests; garden yield; fields and foliage
throat, n.	1789	siren throats	songbird
tooth, n.	373	Garnet Tooth	flames; fire; lava
wagon, n.	16	Seraph's wagon	wings
winged, verbal adj.	483	Winged Beggar	bird
wise, adj.	391	Wise Book	Bible; Old and New Testaments

Appendix D

Table 1.7 Sample of Emily Dickinson's Metonymies

Headword	Franklin	Citation	Interpretation Comments	Year
adder, adj.	1194	Adder's Tongue	venomous snake; [kenning] serpent	1871
Almighty, n.	1148	the Almighty	God; Lord; Heavenly Father (see Job 31:3)	1868
ankle, n.	328	panting Ancle	body walking; person stepping; someone striding	1862
arm, n.	1410	Arm of Chivalry	protection of a knight in armor; [kenning] gallantry	1876
axe, n.	90	An axe shrill singing	person cutting down trees with a sharp instrument	1859
Azof, proper n.	1160	Azof – the Equinox	waves; breakers; the oceans; the deep; water currents of the earth; [historical] pen name of a Civil War correspondent for the 59th regiment of Massachusetts	1869
Baltic, proper n.	1041	Who's Baltic	ocean; great geographic feature; [figurative] source of power	1865
bird, n.	309	Stab the Bird	melody; song; tune; [figurative] happiness; hope; joy; good tidings	1862
Birmingham, proper n.	1407	Birmingham	polished silverware; fine dinner utensils; elegant tools for eating; [kenning] elegance; refinement; gentility	1876
bosom, n.	67	bosom lay	body; physical being; mortal frame (see Proverbs 6:27); [figurative] corpse; cadaver; remains	1859
brow, n.	332	Brow	head; upper half of the human body	1862
Buenos Ayres, proper n.	418	Buenos Ayre	Argentina; Great Britain's sixth dominion	1862

career, n.	1594	The lowliest career	person; worker; mortal; human being; [figurative] biography; lifetime; life span; life story	1882
cart, n.	758	Cart of Butterfly	freight; cargo; [figurative] body; life; moving principle; [kenning] insect flight	1863
cedar, adj.	583	Cedar Floor	neighborhood; community; general public	1863
cedar, adj.	583	Cedar Floor	forest; grove of evergreen trees; [figurative] entire household; whole family	1863
centre, n.	1245	sites of Centres	cluster of dwellings; [kenning] city; village; market; town; community; gathering place	1872
chamber, n.	377	chamber	address; domicile; lodging; residence; dwelling place; [figurative] court; palace; door into heaven; entrance into the Kingdom of God	1862
chatter, n.	543	Chatter	life; communion with the living	1863
chivalry, n.	1410	Arm of Chivalry	a gentleman	1876
Christmas, proper n.	46	Christmas tree	winter holiday in December	1858
church, n.	325	church	whole congregation; [figurative] entire flock; complete fold of sheep; [hypernym] minister; priest; pastor; shepherd; [figurative] worshipper; faithful parishioner; member of a fold; lamb in a flock (see Acts 20:28); [metaphor] corpus; body of Christ (see Colossians 1:24)	1862
clause, n.	1386	clause	law; justice system	1876
closing, n.	564	Closing	sleeping; resting	1863
complexion, n.	171	complexion	skin color	1860

coral, n.	517	Corals	red-tinted reef; [figurative] side of a volcano crater; [metaphor] volatile personality	1863
cornet, n.	406	Cornets	blast of loud music	1862
coronal, n.	722	Coronal	coronation; ceremony of crowning; endowment of a royal status; promotion to a more elevated position; [figurative] garland; wreath of flowers; [metaphor] resurrection; sanctification	1863
cottage, n.	1116	Cottages	town; village; settlement; [figurative] prospects; life-path; lot in life	1865
counter, n.	1134	Counter	accounting; Judgment Day; [figurative] altar; judgment bar	1867
crescent, n.	1453	Crescent	physical body; mortal frame; shell of existence; resemblance of who a person once was; [figurative] face; head	1877
crimson, n.	367	crimson	brightly colored petals	1862
cross, n.	541	Cross' Request	Savior; Redeemer	1863
crown, n.	77	crown	Christ-like suffering; [figurative] funeral pillow; [metaphor] honor; recognition; remembrance; memorial	1859
crucifix, n.	325	Crucifix	cross; burden; persecution; tribulation (see Matthew 27:31-32; 2 Thessalonians 1:4); [figurative] agony; anguish; wound; stigmata; experience of most profound sorrow; [metaphor] grief; heartache; broken heart; loss of a loved one; separation from one's beloved	1862

date, n.	1453	Dates	descendant; posterity; people with future death-day headstone inscriptions	1877
day, n.	1169	Days	human being; mortal individual; deceased person	1870
deck, n.	325	Decks	boat; vessel; watercraft	1862
degree, n.	551	Degree	climate zone; geographic area	1863
door, n.	44	door	house; home; habitation; location; dwelling place	1858
door, n.	75	chamber door	burial place; [figurative] headstone; grave marker	1859
drop, n.	388	drop – of India	moment; time; season; [metaphor] gem; tear-shaped jewel; [figurative] muse; poetic fluency; flow of beautiful language; [kenning] beloved	1862
duck, n.	764	Eider Duck's	feathers; soft covering; [kenning] protection	1863
dust, n.	1575	Dust	physical body; mortal shell	1882
ear, n.	27	ears	body; human being	1858
earth, n.	1	Earth	creation; [personification] Mother Nature	1850
eye, n.	110	eyes	being; creature; [figurative] people; person; individual; human being	1859
eye, n.	216	eyes	body without life force; corpse without vitality	1861
fabric, n.	1466	Fabrics	physical body; [figurative] broken heart; mortal person; human being	1878
face, n.	266	face	being; essence; resurrected body	1861
fainting, verbal adj.	982	fainting	baby; fledgling; [figurative] hungry	1865
feather, n.	1448	feather	bird; flying creature	1877

flood, n.	1207	Floods	totality; everything; all-encompassing life force; [figurative] baptism; sacrament; purification; sanctification; blessing; breath of life	1871
floor, n.	1337	Floor	bottom of an archive; repository; storehouse; [figurative] mental and emotional depths	1874
foot, n.	61	foot	soul; body; upright self	1859
foot, n.	13	feet	meter; metrical unit; numerical measurement in verse; combination of stressed and unstressed syllables in the line of a lyric; [figurative] dancer; dance of blessed spirits	1858
fuzz, n.	1426	Fuzz	field of flowers; [figurative] pollen; plant nectar	1877
gambrel, n.	466	Gambrels	heavenly body; [figurative] arch; dome; firmament; tree; branch; bent piece of wood; curving overhead structure; [metaphor] limb; bodily appendage	1862
Genesis, proper n.	1598	Genesis	the Fall	1883
geography, n.	1691	Geography	earth science textbook	undated
guinea, n.	12	guinea	wealth; treasure	1858
guitar, n.	1403	Guitar	music; melody; poetry; [figurative] essence; substance; creation	1876
hand, n.	72	Hands	person employed to work	1859
head, n.	158	head	deceased person; [figurative] bloom; blossom; seed pod of a flowering plant	1860

hoof, n.	164	hoofs	leg of a quadruped; [metaphor] mount; racing animal; beast that a person travels with (see Isaiah 5:28)	1860
icicle, n.	556	Icicle	winter; [metaphor] sharp, obvious grief; evidence of shedding tears	1863
jewel, n.	1	jewel	adornment; wedding ring; piece of jewelry	1850
joint, n.	291	Joint	rows of a field; shallow valleys formed into farmland for the seeding process	1862
key, n.	431	key	access; control; power of custody; admission by possession of the keys for any place	1862
Kidderminster, proper n.	510	Kidderminster	kidder cloth; reversible double-sided woven goods	1863
knee, n.	237	knee	leg; bottom limb	1861
knee, n.	1330	Knee	worship; adoration; [figurative] attitude of supplication; position of submission	1874
Lapland, proper n.	400	Lapland's	mortality; life on earth; [metaphor] language; scripture; literature; lyric poetry; effective written discourse; [synonym] New England; North America; the New World; [figurative] solitude; seclusion; reticence; modesty; simplicity of motive; purity of heart	1862
lash, n.	1096	Lash	snake; serpent; [figurative] quick movement; sudden flash; potential danger	1865
latitude, n.	125	latitudes	place; land; geographic location	1859

lip, n.	16	lips	person singing; choir member	1858
lip, n.	126	lips	person thirsting	1859
lip, n.	205	Lips	body; self; person; individual human being	1861
load, n.	537	Load	wagon; cart carrying a large amount of coal	1863
long, adv.	1768	long	extensive time period	undated
loom, n.	61	Loom	daily labor; earthly endeavors; mortal life	1859
lute, n.	905	Lutes	bard; poet; troubadour; minstrel; oracle; prophet; author of scripture text; [metaphor] human beings; mortal tabernacles; [figurative] humanities; fine arts; liberal arts; classical learning	1865
man, n.	788	Man	society; civilization	1863
noon, n.	114	noon	life; mortality; earthly existence	1859
north, n.	319	North	place in the sky where the northern lights appear	1862
north, n.	520	North	winter; freezing weather	1863
physiognomy, n.	1372	Physiognomy	mortal; human being	1875
pinion, n.	1448	Pinions	wing; organ of flight	1877
plank, n.	1199	Planks	ship; boat; sea-going vessel; [figurative] thin, flat blade of grass	1871
porch, n.	916	Porch	house; cottage; home; abode; residence; lodging; dwelling place; [figurative] casket; grave; tomb; sepulchre; burial vault	1865
rune, n.	402	Rune	spell; chant; incantation; invocation	1862

screw, n.	293	Screw	body; physical being; material essence; [figurative] nerve; sinew; tendon	1862
seat, n.	1594	seat	destiny; future; mansion	1882
second, n.	425	Second	brief lifetime	1862
sentence, n.	1268	sentence	text; discourse; writing	1872
sepulchre, n.	965	Sepulchre	graveyard; cemetery	1865
shore, n.	178	shore	nation; country; state; commonwealth	1860
sinew, n.	492	Sinew	arm; [figurative] aid; help; service; backup	1862
slipper, n.	19	slipper	person; being; creature; [metaphor] blossom; bloom; type of flower	1858
sod, n.	79	sod	planting bed	1859
sowing, n.	787	Sowing	bouquet; garden flowers; [wordplay] sewing; stitchery; cloth put together with thread; [metaphor] compositions; poetry	1863
supper, n.	1064	Supper	diet; daily bread	1865
surge, n.	203	surge	sea; ocean near the shore	1861
tar, n.	1599	Tar	tarpaulin; canvas; water-proofed clothes of a seafarer; [wordplay] sailor; [metaphor] pall; funeral shroud	1883
thill, n.	758	Thill of Bee	sting [figurative] path; route; track; [kenning] beeline	1863
thorn, n.	267	Thorns	crown; circlet of plaited thorns; spiked wreath similar to the one on the head of Jesus to mock him (see Matthew 27:29); [metaphor] wound; bruise; [figurative] affliction; trial; trouble	1861

Dickinson's Breath of Life

throat, n.	1663	Throat	head	1884
toe, n.	351	Toes	feet; [metaphor] wing	1862
tomb, n.	1210	Tomb	graveyard; [figurative] funeral ceremony; burial service; death procession	1871
vane, n.	306	Vane	weather; temperature; meteorological conditions; wind direction	1862
vanished, verbal adj.	180	vanished	deceased; pertaining to someone long dead; [figurative] outmoded; outdated	1860
violet, n.	442	Violet	rainbow; the chromatic scale; colors in the bandwidth of infracted light	1862
violin, n.	607	Violin	musical instrument; [metaphor] poetry; poetic voice; creative writing; gift of writing verse	1863
visage, n.	1378	Visage	aspect; appearance; true identity	1875
visage, n.	1542	visage	presence; being (see Isaiah 52:14); [figurative] smile	1881
vision, n.	428	Vision	eyes	1862
wardrobe, n.	325	Wardrobe	body; embodiment; incarnation; corporeal presence; physical manifestation in the flesh	1862
wheel, n.	573	Wheels	carriage; wagon; vehicle; conveyance; means of transportation; [metaphor] world; planet; star; universe; heavenly body; [figurative] orbit; round; circuit; circumference; course; destiny; fate; fortune; circular path	1863
whip, n.	1096	Whip	snake; serpent; [figurative] quick movement; sudden flash; potential danger	1865

wifehood, n.	267	Wifehood	matrimony; wedlock; union; legal marriage; consummated love; [figurative] redemption; paradisiacal glory; heavenly bliss; fulfillment of promises; union of body, spirit, heart, and mind through the resurrection	1861
window pane, n.	182	window pane	house; building	1860
worm, n.	110	Worm	butterfly	1859

Works Cited

The following abbreviations are used to refer to the writings of Emily Dickinson:

Fr   *The Poems of Emily Dickinson*, edited by R. W. Franklin, Harvard UP, 1998. Citation by poem number.

L   *The Letters of Emily Dickinson*, edited by Thomas H. Johnson and Theodora Ward, Harvard UP, 1958. Citation by letter number.

Becker, Alton. *Beyond Translation*. U of Michigan P, 2000.

Bianchi, Martha Dickinson. *Emily Dickinson Face to Face: Unpublished Letters with Notes and Reminiscences*. Houghton Mifflin, 1932.

Brashear, Lucy. "'Awake ye muses nine': Emily Dickinson's Prototype Poem." *South Atlantic Bulletin*, vol. 45, no. 4, November 1980, pp. 90–99.

Eberwein, Jane. *Dickinson: Strategies of Limitation*. U of Massachusetts P, 1985.

Emily Dickinson Lexicon website, Brigham Young University, 2007, http://edl.byu.edu/index.php.

Gura, Philip F. *The Wisdom of Words: Language, Theology, and Literature in the New England Renaissance*. Wesleyan UP, 1981.

Juhasz, Suzanne. "The Irresistible Lure of Repetition and Dickinson's Poetics of Analogy." *The Emily Dickinson Journal*, vol. 9, no. 2, 2000, pp. 23–31.

Knox, Helene Margrethe. *The Alien Dimension: A Study of Metaphor and Metonymy in the Poetry of Emily Dickinson*. University of California, Berkeley: ProQuest Dissertations Publishing, 1979, pp. 17–26, 74, 98, 109.

McMahon, April M. S. *Understanding Language Change*. Cambridge UP, 1994.

Newman, Samuel Phillips. *A Practical System of Rhetoric*. Dayton and Newman, 1842.

Romney, Rebecca. "Word-Weaving: Kennings in Emily Dickinson's Poems." Kyoto, Japan: Emily Dickinson International Society conference, August 2007.

Rossetti, Christina G. *Sing-Song: A Nursery-Rhyme Book*. George Routledge and Sons, 1872.

Sewall, Richard B. *The Lyman Letters: New Light on Emily Dickinson and Her Family*. U of Massachusetts P, 1965.

Short, Bryan. "Emily Dickinson and the Origins of Language." *The Emily Dickinson Journal*, vol. 9, no. 2, 2000, pp. 109–119.

Steiner, George. *After Babel: Aspects of Language and Translation* [1975]. Oxford UP, 1992.

Thoreau, Henry David. "Walden, 1854." *The Portable Thoreau*, edited by Carl Bode, Penguin Books, 1987.

Watkins, Calvert. *How to Kill a Dragon: Aspects of Indo-European Poetics*. Oxford UP, 1995.

Webster, Noah. *An American Dictionary of the English Language*, 2 vol. reprint of the 1841 edition, Adams Brothers, 1844. Online renovated edition at http://edl.byu.edu/webster.

Werning, Marcus. "The 'Complex First' Paradox: Why Do Semantically Thick Concepts So Early Lexicalize as Nouns?" *Interaction Studies*, vol. 9, no. 1, 2008, pp. 67–83.

Whitman, Walt. "Slang in America." *Prose Works 1892*, vol. II, edited by Floyd Stovall, New York UP, 1963.

Further Reading

Bennett, Fordyce R. *A Reference Guide to the Bible in Emily Dickinson's Poetry*. Scarecrow Press, 1997.

Benvenuto, Richard. "Words Within Words: Dickinson's Use of the Dictionary." *ESQ*, vol. 29, 1983, pp. 46–55.

Buckingham, Willis J. "Emily Dickinson's Dictionary." *Harvard Library Bulletin*, vol. 25, 1977, pp. 489–92.

Budick, E. Miller. *Emily Dickinson and the Life of Language: A Study in Symbolic Poetics*. Louisiana State UP, 1985.

Burbick, Joan. "The Irony of Self-Reference: Emily Dickinson's Pronominal Language." *Essays in Literature*, vol. 9, no. 1, Spring 1982, pp. 83–95.

Cuddy, Lois A. "The Latin Imprint on Emily Dickinson's Poetry: Theory and Practice." *American Literature*, vol. 50, no. 1, March 1978, pp. 74–84.

"Emily Dickinson's Schooling: Amherst Academy." *The Emily Dickinson Museum*, https://www.emilydickinsonmuseum.org/emily-dickinson/biography/special-topics/emily-dickinsons-schooling-amherst-academy/.

Freeman, Margaret H. "Metaphor Making Meaning: Dickinson's Conceptual Universe." *Journal of Pragmatics*, vol. 24, no. 6, 1995, pp. 643–666.

Garland, Katherine. "Noah Webster's House – 46 Main Street." *Amherst Historic*, http://amhersthistoric.org/items/show/4.

Hagenbüchle, Roland. "Emily Dickinson's Poetic Covenant." *The Emily Dickinson Journal*, vol. 2, no. 2, 1993, pp. 14–39.

Hamilton, Craig. "A Cognitive Rhetoric of Poetry and Emily Dickinson." *Language and Literature: International Journal of Stylistics*, vol. 13, no. 3, August 2005, pp. 279–294.

Howard, William. "Emily Dickinson's Poetic Vocabulary." *PMLA*, vol. 72, no. 1, March 1957, pp. 225–248.

Hubbard, Melanie. "The Word Made Flesh: Dickinson's Variants and the Life of Language." *Dickinson's Fascicles: A Spectrum of Possibilities*, edited by Paul Crumbley and Eleanor Elson Heginbotham, Ohio State UP, 2014, pp. 33–62.

Lindberg-Seyersted, Brita. *The Voice of the Poet: Aspects of Style in the Poetry of Emily Dickinson*. Harvard UP, 1968.

Miller, Cristanne. *Emily Dickinson: A Poet's Grammar*. Harvard UP, 1987.

Monte, Steven. "Dickinson's Searching Philology." *The Emily Dickinson Journal*, vol. 12, no. 2, 2003, pp. 21–51.

Ross, Christine. "Uncommon Measures: Emily Dickinson's Subversive Prosody." *The Emily Dickinson Journal*, vol. 10, no. 1, 2001, pp. 70–98.

Scheurer, Erika. "'Near, but remote': Emily Dickinson's Epistolary Voice." *The Emily Dickinson Journal*, vol. 4, no. 1, 1995, pp. 86–107.

Sharon-Zisser, Shirley. "To 'See – Comparatively': Emily Dickinson's Use of Simile." *The Emily Dickinson Journal*, vol. 3, no. 1, 1994, pp. 59–84.

Small, Judy Jo. *Positive as Sound: Emily Dickinson's Rhyme*. U of Georgia P, 1990.

Trench, Richard Chenevix. *On the Study of Words*. 22nd edition [1851–52]. Macmillan, 1892.

Chapter 2

"Syllables of Velvet, Sentences of Plush": Emily Dickinson as Polyglot

Nicole Panizza
Coventry University

Abstract

The enigmatic allure of language, as a critical means of identification and exploration, remained a primary force throughout Emily Dickinson's life. Her perceptive and innovative use of poetic space, sound, and impetus established a resonance and commune with her immediate environs, which can be viewed as proceeding from a profoundly musical sensibility. When acknowledging the self-conscious use of music in Dickinson's poetry, both as a source of imagery and as a strategy for shaping her terse, condensed poetic line, music provided the ground on which the superstructure of her poetic thought was built and a condition of being toward which it aspired. This essay investigates Dickinson's intersections with music and text as bilingual practice. It addresses her innovative use of musical device, metaphor, and rudiment as an expression of her desire to communicate with, and connect to, diverse and disparate domains.

Key words: music, poetic sound, jazz, nineteenth-century music books

***

> Music expresses that which cannot be said and on which it is impossible to be silent.
>
> Victor Hugo

Emily Dickinson loved language, not only for its practical properties, or as an essential communicative tool, but as the conduit for her private, radical manifesto; she tasted words, savoring their unique sound, length, "beat," and shape. Dickinson wrestled with, and luxuriated in, the plush interior corridors of the phonological and syntactical qualities of language; language was her religion, her lover, her *raison d'être*. The notion of Emily Dickinson as polyglot implies that she had knowledge of, and moved between, many languages.

While interest in her use of the English vernacular endures, this was not her sole form of creative communication. The ways in which she conveyed information, thought, and feeling traversed many platforms and obstacles. Her inventive approach to the articulation of the human condition remains a critical example of her inclusive creative acumen. Dickinson strategically drew inspiration from many sources: the domestic space, nature, religion, sociopolitical constructs, and her own imagination. She proceeded as not only a multilingual artist but as an inventor of a new language: a scribe of the glossopoetic. In the act of repositioning her relationship to language, she emerged as an unparalleled wordsmith and a master in the art of minimalist storytelling. Coded idiom was her speciality—to "Tell all the truth but tell it slant" (Fr1263).

According to Bryan Short, "Emily Dickinson's intellectual milieu devoted considerable attention to the origins and development of language" (109). Throughout her formative years, she was exposed to etymological and phonemic orthographical aspects of the written and spoken word. She read widely and absorbed the contexts from which language derived and in which it dwelled. This provided her with the tools to extend her relationship with language beyond prescribed expectations and therefore enabled her to (re)create her literary legacy. As an elucidation of this concept, Short states that "Consideration of the origins of language permits us to see her as a master of rather than an escapee from the history she bent to her extraordinary poetic purposes" (115). One of the poet's main sources for lingual material was through the servants in her family home. While there was a clear expectation that she would learn examples from the standard modern languages of the day (French and German), she was also exposed to Hiberno-English and the "'songified' quality of African American Vernacular English" (Murray 123). The Hiberno-English accent, most notably registered through Dickinson's close relationship with Mrs. Rosina Mack and Margaret "Maggie" Maher, her Irish servants, included extra vowels between certain consonants (syllabification of liquids, namely the letters *l* and *r*), which made it easier, and more swift, to communicate. "English words were merely superimposed on a substratum of Gaelic syntax" (120). Dickinson was also heavily influenced by the aural nuances of "the work of Scottish peasant poet Robert Burns, who mixed Scots English with his mother tongue, the Lallans dialect, to exciting linguistic effect" (120).

The ways in which Emily Dickinson interacted with language, particularly her "unconventional manipulation of words and meaning, figurative language, syntactic structures, and rhetorical strategies" (White 38), established a mode of practice that immediately lends itself to the possibility of polylingual engagement and treatment. Dickinson's punctuation, distinctive rhythmic meters, and sense of prosody mirror the inherent lyric nature of musical language and practice. She was aware of this symbiotic relationship and used it to great effect in her poems and letters. Dickinson's prolific use of the dash has long been an area of scholarly interest. Ellen Louise Hart, for example, states that "[the] dashes serve multiple, sometimes oppositional purposes, as critics have shown: making syntactic connections, letting meaning resonate, allowing sound to echo, introducing silence, acting as a musical rest, or permitting a breath" (218). Through music, Dickinson was exposed to a language that could articulate where words could only go so far; a language that gave character and life force to her punctuation, epitomized her syncopated rhythmic "cells," and provided a rich world of color, texture, and depth from which to paint her texts. An expansion thematic material pertaining to identity, performance, and narration were now made possible. Elizabeth Phillips, in her book *Emily Dickinson: Personae and Performance*, refers to Dickinson's affinity with musical timing, instinct, intimacy, and lyric presence: "The speech is often colloquial but also personal . . . There are so many 'performances' in the poems that Dickinson may elude us. Adopting provisional attitudes and myriad voices, she changes point of view, role, situation, genre, language, and style with remarkable speed and adroitness" (78).

Emily Dickinson's conscious engagement with, and application of, the language of music creates a persuasive argument for her also assuming a role of creative translator. The merging (and, in some cases, substitution) of words for musical terminology and her use of music in a metaphoric and imagistic capacity raise interesting questions about the many ways in which complementary prosodic platforms can support and enhance the poetry's inherent musical genetic material. Ana Luísa Amaral argues that:

> Translating poetry requires both a deep knowledge of the original language and of the poem's historical, cultural, and literary context; more than anything, though, it requires a still deeper knowledge of the language into which it's being translated, the translator's own language. Added to this must be a love of that language, the language of the person receiving and then transforming the poem into a new poem—creating a new path.

By amalgamating her unique, laser-sharp literary acumen with her knowledge of music theory and practice, Emily Dickinson established a fluid, non-doctrinal linguistic ecosystem. Her ability to ascertain balance, ratio, and creative synergy between distinct forms of communication cemented the notion of her ability to proceed "polyglotally." However, to understand the true extent of her polylingual practice, one must connect with her biography, observe her literary evolution, and, critically, trace her close relationship to the language of music.

Spatial Improvisations – Emily Dickinson's "Lyric Communications"

Music and poetry share a long history, which is revealed in the words used to describe the two forms of art. For example, Cerys Matthews explains that the "Welsh word 'cerdd' can be translated as either 'verse' or 'music.'" This "binary" expression draws on the rich tradition of the troubadour, the performing minstrel who viewed the relationship between text and music as vital and organically symbiotic. Their creative practice, intimately connected to the various resonances between the two (seemingly disparate) art forms, inherently promoted the combined power of this plurality. They lived through the truth of this union: the connection between lyric poetry and musical idiom as an inescapable truth.

When considering the well-documented history of the lyric within poetic praxis and consciousness, it can be argued that Emily Dickinson was following a celebrated lineage of poets who were drawn to the act of creating a singular, emotionally generated product. Cristanne Miller, in her 1987 book *Emily Dickinson: A Poet's Grammar,* posits Dickinson's lyric contingencies as providing the poet "with the linguistic and psychological freedom she needs to express, or inscribe, herself" (18). In Miller's view, the act of "enacting" the lyric enabled Dickinson to "articulate chaotic or rebellious feeling and thought" (12). Dickinson's technique of instilling a feeling of connection to the human and the familiar, while concurrently "improvising" within contemporary ideology, establishes an undeniable link with the act of music theory and praxis. When reflecting on this strategic alignment—between lyric sensibility and agency and the ways in which she adapted her verse to support her very personal manifesto—one must also trace Dickinson's intimate relationship to music. It is then that we begin to digest fully her ease of movement between these two languages. It is difficult to pinpoint which route had the most influence on her work; it most likely involved a hybrid of many routes. In seeking to elucidate the role that the language of music played in her life, I start from the point of its conception and construction.

Dickinson's Music Training

The earliest account of Emily Dickinson's relationship to music can be traced back to 1832. At the tender age of two and a half, according to her Aunt Lavinia (Mrs. Loring Norcross), Dickinson referred to her explorations of the piano as "the moosic."[1] Records suggest that Dickinson continued to be fascinated with music throughout her childhood, and, as was commonplace for a young

---

[1] Lavinia's description of Dickinson is found in Johnson's notes to Letter 11; see page 33 in Johnson.

woman of her social milieu, she was encouraged to pursue the study of it in both theory and practice. Dickinson's main music tuition derived from a rigorous level of training as part of her primary and secondary education. In 1840, she joined Amherst Academy. She remained a student there for the next seven years and, as part of her enrollment, underwent an extremely regimented education that consisted of both science and humanities-based subjects, such as German, Latin, biology, geology, history, and philosophy. The study of music also played a role in her formal education schedule and remained a point of dedicated interest outside of this framework. When at home during term breaks (and throughout various bouts of illness that necessitated her return home), Dickinson continued her music study, in addition to other pursuits such as botany, cooking, daily exercise, and language and singing lessons.

While at Amherst Academy, Emily Dickinson formed what would be a notable friendship, particularly in musical terms. Abiah Root joined Amherst Academy in June 1844 and left in February 1845, which is when the two began exchanging letters. Both young women shared a love of the piano and corresponded about this on a regular basis. A surprisingly large number of these letters specify Dickinson's personal approach to music theory and praxis, representing a significant opportunity to better understand the role that music played in her life. Concerned that she would not fall behind her competitor, she wrote to Root in 1845 that "Father intends to have a piano very soon. How happy I shall be when I have one of my own!" (L6). Within a few months, her hopes were rewarded. The summer of 1845 was a notably happy one for Dickinson, with the arrival of the greatly anticipated piano. A gift from her father, the "old-fashioned square piano in an elaborately carved mahogany case" (Bianchi 34) was intended for use by the entire family. However, she seems to have adopted it as her own. She writes to Root in August 1845 about her lessons with Aunt Selby, who was staying with the Dickinson family throughout the summer months. This would have provided an ideal opportunity for her to extend her knowledge of the piano and to develop her skills without the added distraction of formal academic study: "I am taking [piano] lessons this term, of Aunt Selby who is spending the summer with us. I never enjoyed myself more . . . I have the same Instruction book that you have, Bertini, and I am getting along in it very well" (L7). In 1846, Dickinson tells Root that "I take music lessons and practise two hours in a day" (L9), and "I have been learning a beautiful thing, which I long to have you hear" (L12). Upon completion of her intermediate studies at Amherst Academy in 1847, Emily Dickinson transferred her final stage of formal education to Mount Holyoke Seminary, where she remained for approximately 11 months. Heavily steeped in religious doctrine and moral expectation, the students were worked extremely hard and regularly drilled in academic rigor and discipline. Despite Dickinson returning home for a short period due to illness, she immersed herself in her studies. One of the many benefits of her final year of schooling was the opportunity to extend her musical education. While the time available for music practice was increasingly marginalized (due to the scope and nature of her academic work), she still managed to participate in one of the two school choirs, undertook regular singing training, and continued to devote time to her pianistic development: "from 1½ until 2 I sing in Seminary Hall. From 2¾ until 3¾. I practise upon the Piano" (L18).

While a notable level of musical training stemmed directly from the educational domain, Dickinson also pursued other musical activity and outlet. One of the most critical examples of Dickinson's early music training was her involvement in a local Sunday evening singing group. An extension to her assumed involvement with her family's church, the First Congregational Church, this aspect of her musical development was on a more social scale. It was here that Dickinson had the freedom to explore repertoire (albeit based on religious texts and themes) beyond the strict musical doctrines within the church service itself. In February 1845, Dickinson wrote to Root, explaining that she attends these weekly rehearsals "to improve my voice" (L5). Religious tradition and practice were very much established familial and community-based activities during Dickinson's formative years. Raised as a New England Calvinist, she was not only expected to adhere to daily religious ritual within the home (group prayer, readings, catechism) but was also expected to attend regular church services in her hometown of Amherst, Massachusetts. These involved a requisite immersion in the study and practice of hymnal technique and related performance-based traditions, where the use of music was controlled and, to some extent, prescribed. The sheer level of exposure to a breadth of hymnal content—the incessant, quasi-hypnotic level of required repetition combined with more traditional, idiomatic tropes regarding musical inflection versus textual order—no doubt supplied Dickinson with vital musical fodder, serving as an inspiration for her future literary practice. While Dickinson proceeded to reject formal religious practice, she remained devoted to a deeper questioning of the human aspects of religious experience as doctrine: life, death, and eternity. For Dickinson, the search for a deeper meaning of spirituality became an insistent and recurring theme. Music remained an inseparable aspect of this quest and a necessary mode of personal expression.

An evitable outcome of this degree of immersion in religious practice was her development in both the knowledge and practice of the hymn. During the time of Dickinson's youth, America was undergoing a Protestant religious revival. Emerging in the late eighteenth century and extending to the 1850s, this was known as the Second Great Awakening, and interest in and dedication to religious practice became more prolific across the United States. New England saw a steep rise in church service attendance, with new "orders" established.

The more purist traits of early American Calvinism (such as personal review, penance, and salvation only through God) gave way to a more optimistic, "liberal" view that focused more on humans' abilities to change their lives for the better. Women represented the majority of converts during the early 1800s, perhaps due to increased economic insecurity and as an assertion of self beyond the instilled patriarchal rule. America continued to draw heavily on the Anglo-hymn tradition, none more so than on the hymnody of Isaac Watts.

Isaac Watts's hymns were already an established part of daily religious practice in America by the time Dickinson was born in 1830. Watts produced his hymn output alone and demonstrated a determination to seek "a new relationship between church song and scripture," arising from his "refusal to accept scripture without altering it, [and] from his determination to interpret its relevance to present experience" (England 126). In this sense, Watts preempted Dickinson's own search for personal emancipation through the act of lingual (re)construction. In Watts, Dickinson found "a model both pious and adventurous—a kindred spirit who encouraged her own bold exploration and experimentation" (126). Dickinson's knowledge of Watts's hymns began from early childhood. Standard New England hymn books largely drew from Watts's canon, namely *The Psalms of David Imitated in the Language of the New Testament and Spiritual Songs* (written by Watts in 1719). This hymn book could be found in every New England school, church, and household, and it served as the primary hymn reference of the time. The presence of Watts in the Dickinson family is clear from their library, which included *Watts Psalms* (1810),[2] Watts's *Christian Psalmody in Four Parts* (1817),[3] and *The Psalms, Hymns, and Spiritual Songs of the Rev. Isaac Watts, D.D.* (1834).[4] These three volumes represent the key hymnodic influences during Dickinson's early years. The "performance" of Watts's hymns, designed to be sung *a cappella*, was subject to a range of directives drawn from indicative marking within the hymnal itself. Samuel Worcester, in the Preface to *The Psalms, Hymns, and Spiritual Songs of the Rev. Isaac Watts*,[5] asserted that the performance of Watts's hymnody, if "entitled to be

---

[2] The copy that belonged to the Dickinson family is inscribed "E. Dickinson" in pencil and "Emily Norcross Book" in ink and was called *Watts Psalms carefully suited to the Christian Worship in the United States of America;* it is bound with *Hymns and Spiritual Songs*, 1810. Numerous pages have the top corner folded; see EDR 7 at Harvard's Houghton Library.

[3] Harvard's Houghton Library records that this book is inscribed as belonging to Edward Dickinson, but the book is not housed at Houghton.

[4] Samuel Worcester, D. D., wrote the directions for musical expression in this edition, which was edited by his son, Samuel M. Worcester, professor of rhetoric at Amherst College; see Houghton's EDR 339.

[5] Samuel M. Worcester's Preface to the 1834 edition owned by the Dickinson family reprints the Preface from earlier editions, which had been written by his father.

called good," relied almost exclusively on "the movement, quantity, and tone of voice" being "well adapted to the general subject, and so varied as justly to express the different thoughts, sentiments, and passions" (v–vi).

The hymns that Emily Dickinson became immersed in (and countless others of her age) followed a lineage of English hymnody tradition. In structural terms, Watts merged extant scripture with what is now deemed "hymn form": a lyrical quatrain based on traditional English folk literature, consisting of four lines of alternating rhyme in either *abab* or *xaxa* configuration. As a general rule, Watts's three favored forms were:

Common Meter	featuring alternating lines of iambic tetrameter with iambic trimeter (8.6.8.6)
Long Meter	solely iambic tetrameter (8.8.8.8)
Short Meter	two lines of iambic trimeter, followed by one line of iambic tetrameter, concluding with one line of iambic trimeter (6.6.8.6)[6]

They also contained key musical "markers" that denoted specific directives regarding expression and musical gesture. The use of Roman-lettered vowels denoted dynamic movement:

a	very slow
e	slow
i	common
o	quick
u	very quick

Other expressions suggested suitable tempo and mood:

p – *pathetic*	slow-soft
g – *grand*	slow-loud
b – *beautiful*	quick-soft
s – *spirited*	quick-loud

---

[6] All denote syllables per line.

"Some passages require not any considerable change from the common, either in movement or quantity; but either a peculiar *distinctness* of utterance, or some peculiar *distinction* in the tone or modulation of voice. This expression, or rather these varieties of expression, are denoted by the letter d" (vii). Further, noting issues of punctuation, Worcester states that

> regard has been had to musical expression. In some instances, therefore, different points or pauses are inserted, from what would have been used, had the grammatical construction, only, been regarded. The *dash* is intended to denote an expressive suspension. In order to good expression, a distinct and judicious observance of the pauses, is absolutely necessary. (vii)

While many writers have been drawn to the relationship between Dickinson's direct engagement with Watts's compositions and her undeniable use of hymn meter within her own literary process, can we say that she did so *consciously*? Perhaps. What is worthy of closer scrutiny is not so much her faithful regard for Watts's material, but more what she imagined and actioned within these seemingly strict, orthodox boundaries.

This signature technique is also evident in her approach to the "lyric strain." If the lyric's "defining characteristic is the priority of its sonic pattern, then it depends on being *heard*: it hangs everything on the presence and engagement of its audience . . . a social context of which the writer is a part" (Willis 229–230). Strategic connection with issues of identity, and the sonic properties embedded within lyric texts, became an instinctive and natural facet of Dickinson's artistic *raison d'être*: the act of lyric construction, expressly as a "language-based, rhythmical space for the viable [and universal]—as part of a cultural and historical process, creating 'ontological openings'" (Miller, *Reading in Time*, 47).

Her relationship to lyric verse began from a young age, initially drawing on a core foundation of what was common nineteenth-century lyric practice: "the majority of nineteenth-century verse maintained a type of diction, syntax, and descriptive detail that sounded stilted or overblown to the twentieth-century ear" (22), and poems "blended lyric and narrative properties in various ways" (23). The late eighteenth-century ballad revival in Britain was a key factor in shaping the Romantic poetry of that time; it was a popular framework for "imitation and experimentation" (49) and (in Blake's words) a means of "emancipating 'new poets'" (50). Extended lyric works, such as Tennyson's *Evangeline* (1847) and Longfellow's *Hiawatha* (1855), became increasingly popular in the United States during Dickinson's formative years and provided a fertile (if somewhat restrictive) ground from which to cultivate the basis of her lyric technique. Dickinson's immersion in the work of Elizabeth Barrett Browning, notably *The Poet's Vows* (1836), *A Vision of Poets* (1844), and *Aurora Leigh* (1856), one of her favorite works, offered an invaluable corridor of entry to social and gender commentary within contemporary lyric practice. While examples reflecting political and social reform (such as abolition) were plentiful, disparate associations between gender and literary production (and, indeed, publication) were also notably apparent: "Gender association with the lyric functioned differently for men like Longfellow or Whittier, who had an investment in the public status of the profession of the poet, and for women like Dickinson, for whom there was no question of public professionalism" (26).

Based on details contained in her letters and in her poems about poetry, "Dickinson regarded the poet as powerful and poetry as an expression rivaling divine epiphany in its ability to inspire, not as effeminate" (26). Her tendency toward those writers who dared to query the status quo of contemporary poetics, and her fascination with the ways in which they explored and developed these tensions in written form, provided the impetus to experiment with shorter lyric forms that still retained "sonic impact," particularly in relation to her innovative approach to "structural, aural, rhythmic, [and] syntactical patterning" (38). While her lyric tendencies may have arguably "linked Dickinson, in her writing practice, not just to other women who wrote poetry in her age, or to those men and women to whom she mailed poems, but generically with the wide range of poets she had read who were also experimenting with lyric verse" (48), Dickinson emerged as a poet who "found it fruitful and inspiring to work out from communal norms, shared rhythms of thought and expression, and well-known 'tunes' in creating her own distinctive poems" (81). A "poet of sounds" (45), she defiantly navigated her own compositional rite of passage. Her subliminal response to issues of assonance, word rhythm, space, pause, punctuated reference and utterance, melodic contour, and performative gesture can be clearly traced back to lyric tradition and Watts's legacy, acknowledging a keen eye for creativity with boundary, while simultaneously violating its inherent foundational code.

Through her strategic management of lyric contingency and Watts's hymns, she experienced firsthand the "bilingual" nature of the text-music partnership. The lyric tradition and the ways in which Watts conceived and shaped his compositions "became involved with Emily Dickinson's vocal cords, fingers, diaphragm, and lungs very early in her life" (England 85). Her innate ability (and, arguably, one of her greatest accomplishments) was to "recognize the possibilities for an ambitious, complex, and powerfully expressive [form of] lyric poetry—departing altogether from the hymn and ballad forms [she] heard as a foundation for nature's and her own meter" (81).

Dickinson's Music-Making in the Home

Once Emily Dickinson left Mount Holyoke Seminary, the domestic space soon became a primary point of arrival and departure, a creative lab and private stage. It was here that she dared to more formally consider music and poetry as a symbiotic necessity. The daily ritual of domestic activity mirrored the repetitive action of artistic production. To ensure that creative space was available to her, she fashioned a life of interiority. According to Diana Fuss, "Dickinson's critics all seem to agree that interiority, modeled on the architectural space of tomb or prison, was the necessary prerequisite for her poetry" (3). Her approach was one of calculated strategy: a quest for personal emancipation derived from the careful control of her relationship to language within the domestic space.

Emily Dickinson's working day was based on routine and a certain degree of inevitable boredom. The family home represented comfort but also challenge. Dickinson was expected to contribute to the efficient running of the home and, as a direct result, was conversant in the many languages required to communicate responsibility, trust, engagement, and connection within the domestic space. Her daily routine consisted of cooking, cleaning, sewing, gardening, reading, receiving guests (friends and family), prayer, exercise, and writing letters; she embraced some of these duties more willingly than others. It also involved regular music practice, in piano and singing. What is clear is that regardless of the balance of activity on any given day, Dickinson's various duties relied on the act of tactic and repetition. It was through the banal, rote iterations of these actions that she gained valuable knowledge regarding creative process and outcome, which informed how she conceived and curated her creative legacy.

The ways in which Dickinson conceived, drafted, and completed her poetic canon have been extensively documented, as has her approach to domestic chores. In direct alliance with Dickinson's daily acts of repetition were pressing issues of frugality, notation, and annotation. A staple of the Dickinson family library, Lydia Maria Child's orthodox instruction in the manual *The Frugal Housewife*, espoused the critical importance of thoughtful concision: "The true economy of housekeeping is simply the art of gathering up all the fragments, so that nothing be lost. I mean fragments, of *time*, as well as *materials*. Nothing should be thrown away so long as it is possible to make any use of it, however trifling that use may be" (3).[7] Dickinson often wrote on what "fragments" she

---

[7] The Dickinson family copy is inscribed with Dickinson's mother's name and has many indications of use, such as folded corners and pencil markings; see EDR 355 in Harvard's Houghton Library.

could find, such as on random sections and flaps of envelopes, chocolate wrappers, bills, and party invitations. What she wrote ranged from ideas for her next poem, to making notes for ingredients required for the preparation of the evening meal, to the recounting of the latest snatches of insight and information, via letter, to close friends and family. Through her inspired musings, Dickinson became an expert in communicating profound meaning from fragmented sources; the fascination was in the *trajectory* and not merely the end product. While these methodologies are somewhat congruent to the shape of her domestic existence, it is less apparent how her engagement with the *process* of music-making, in some way, mirrored these.

The study and practice of music was a valued activity in the Dickinson household. As a vehicle for intimate communication, it provided the required level of "contribution" regarding expectation versus social etiquette and contributed to familial entertainment. The nature of music development and maturation required Dickinson to acquire a self-directional approach to the art form, from the confines of her domestic space. In some ways, this was more straightforward than contemporary equivalents: music was a principle form of home entertainment, and educational schemes and the sourcing of preferred repertoire became not only a communal desire but a veritable rite of passage for a woman of Dickinson's age and social standing. Once she had left formal education and had returned to her family seat, Dickinson was expected to continue her commitment to music training and scholarship, as was her younger sister Lavinia, although Emily is said to have played the piano "better" (Bingham 153). While she was supportive of Lavinia's studies (gifting her a "first piano piece" "entitled *Home on a Waltz*, an arrangement of *Home Sweet Home*"), she was also prone to sisterly barbs—well-meaning, if impromptu, advice (Leyda 1: 104). Writing to her brother Austin during the summer of 1851, Dickinson declared: "Vinnie is at the instrument, humming a pensive air concerning a young lady who thought she was 'almost there.' Vinnie seems much grieved, and I really suppose *I* ought to betake myself to weeping; I'm pretty sure that I shall if she dont abate her singing" (L42). She was also expected to evidence sufficient progress in her studies by performing to family and close friends, sometimes on demand. A letter from Emily to Abiah Root in 1848 discusses this further: "After our return, Father wishing to hear the Piano, I like an obedient daughter, played & sang a few tunes, much to his apparent gratification. We then retired & the next day & the next were as happily spent as the eventful Thanksgiving day itself" (L20). Music-making within the home, primarily based on social contexts, was a phenomenon that Dickinson was used to and, on occasion, even welcomed. The Dickinsons received guests on a regular basis and, as was customary of the time, were the recipients of impromptu performances that demonstrated the range of musical prowess on offer. When Mabel Loomis Todd visited, for example, Dickinson "listened from the hallway or the top of the stairs. After Beethoven or Bach or Scarlatti, a tray would arrive in the parlor—carried by the housekeeper—with a glass of sherry, a poem from Emily, or a flower from her garden to reward the performance" (McDowell 160).

An equally integral part of Dickinson's musical life in the home was that of her exposure to musical traditions pertaining to the family's servants. She became well-versed in contemporary musical forms (such as minstrel ballads), and those more historic (particularly dances such as the hornpipe, polka, and waltz). She became increasingly interested in European folk tradition, primarily through her relationship to two Irish servants, Mrs. Rosina Mack and Margaret Maher, both of whom were post-famine immigrants hailing from the primarily bilingual catchment of South Tipperary. Her direct immersion in aspects of Irish folklore afforded Dickinson new ways in which to approach the wider nature of creative communication. Her close relationship with Margaret Maher remains a key factor in her polyglottal practice. Not only did Maher bring knowledge of literary craftsmanship to the Homestead (Dickinson wrote drafts of poems in the kitchen and sought Maher's advice once penned), but she also exposed Emily to examples of Irish dance tunes and balladry. While Irish music was widely practiced across all classes in America by the middle of the nineteenth century, issues of fortunate proximity enabled Dickinson to engage with the intimate nature of this form in a deeper way.

Although scant in both scope and number, Emily Dickinson's intersections with the language of music did extend beyond the front parlor and the servants' quarters. Despite her dedication to the training and practice of music, there was "little to inspire or challenge her, for concerts in Amherst were indeed rare" (Whicher 13); as a result, "she did not hear much [music] that was downright bad or much that had particular merit either" (Van Loon 734). However, Dickinson describes her attendance at concert performances in her letters. These attendances were not great in number, but the letters reveal a sustained interest in hearing musical performances throughout her life. In 1846, for example, she found the voices of a group of young singers performing at the Amherst Academy "beautiful . . . and more appropriate for the occasion than band music would have been" (Leyda 1: 120), and in 1853, when the Germanians performed as part of the Spring Exhibition at Amherst College: "The Germanians gave a concert here . . . I never heard [such] *sounds* before. They seemed like *brazen Robins*" (L118). During her trip to Boston in 1846, Dickinson wrote to Abiah Root about attending an exhibit at the Chinese Museum. In keeping with the trend at the time for all things "Oriental," the program featured Chinese musicians playing a variety of compositions. Although Dickinson was unimpressed with the musical abilities of the performer she saw, the event received a rather detailed description in her letter to Abiah:

> Two of the Chinese go with this exhibition. One of them is a Professor of music in China & the other is teacher of a writing school at home. . . . The Musician played upon two of his instruments & accompanied them with his voice. It needed great command over my risible faculty to enable me to keep sober as this amateur was performing, yet he was so very polite to give us some of his native music that we could not do otherwise than to express ourselves highly edified with his performances. (L13)

In July 1851, Emily travelled to Northampton, Massachusetts, with her parents and sister to hear the celebrated "Swedish Nightingale," soprano Jenny Lind. In a letter to Austin, Emily vividly describes the event:

> how Jennie [sic] came out like a child and sang and sang again, how boquets [sic] fell in showers, and the roof was rent with applause . . . how we all loved Jennie Lind, but not accustomed oft to her manner of singing did'nt fancy *that* so well as we did *her* . . . she has an air of *exile* in her mild blue eyes, and a something sweet and touching in her native accent which charms her many friends – "Give me my thatched cottage" as she sang grew so earnest she seemed half lost in song . . . we will talk about her sometime when you come –." (L46)

Dickinson also appreciated the work of Anton Rubinstein. In May 1873, she wrote to her cousin Frances Norcross, "Glad you heard Rubinstein. Grieved Loo [Lavinia] could not hear him. He makes me think of polar nights Captain Hall could tell! Going from ice to ice! What an exchange of awe!" (L390). Judy Jo Small analyzes the significance of a later letter by "Clara Bellinger Green, who recounts a visit made in 1877 after Dickinson asked to hear Clara's sister Nora sing a solo version of the Twenty-third Psalm" (51). Dickinson had listened to Nora sing from upstairs and "then came down to meet the two sisters and their brother in the library and to express her pleasure" (51). Clara recalls Dickinson saying, "I have been long familiar with the voice and laugh of each of you" (51). Clara then alludes to Dickinson's musical aspirations: "after hearing Rubinstein [?]—I believe it was Rubinstein—play in Boston,[8] she had become convinced

---

[8] Small notes, however, that Dickinson "could not have heard Rubinstein perform. He did not come to the United States until 1872, after she had ceased to leave Amherst. . . . She may have attended concerts during other trips to Boston; few letters survive from the months she spent in Boston in 1864 and 1865" (228 n20).

that she could never master the art and had forthwith abandoned it once and for all, giving herself up then wholly to literature" (51). Small explains that Clara's "recollection suggests two rather remarkable things: first, that Dickinson may once have had serious musical ambitions that she relinquished for poetry, and second, that she had an auditory relationship to a town and its people that she had closed out of her sight" (51). The confluence of Emily Dickinson's catalogue of musical experience, training, and exposure to various influences and scenarios rendered her suitable to employ the language of music as a creative device of choice, one arguably equal to her primary poetic aesthetic. One of the most pertinent examples of this symbiotic partnership is in comparative examples of her role as a curator. Naturally adept at the art of design, in both content and proportion (as demonstrated in her Herbarium[9] and, as many manuscript scholars argue, her fascicle project), Emily Dickinson's personal music book provides an equally compelling case for the compilation of music composition as a phonological act.

Bilingual Practice

Emily Dickinson's Music Book[10] (EDR 469) represents a rare opportunity to delve into the poet's musical tastes, preferences, and technical skill; according to George Boziwick, it "opens a significant window into mid-nineteenth-century music-making" (83). The creation and curation of music books (or "folios") was a popular pastime for young middle-to-upper class women during the nineteenth century. The act of sourcing and selecting sheet music demonstrated a keen involvement with the study and practice of music, thereby faithfully adhering to specific, primarily gender-based social norms, and a way in which young women could demonstrate their knowledge of and interest in the most popular tunes of the day. The initial sourcing of material in Dickinson's music book can be traced back to 1843 and is believed to have continued for some eight years, until approximately 1851. The book is believed to have been bound in Boston in 1852, when she was 22 years old, and her curatorial interest in the book was at its height between 1843 and 1845; these inclusions represent more than one-third of the entire collection. These years coincided with her music studies at Amherst Academy and the arrival of her family's piano, which would have also helped to ignite her interest in seeking out new additions to her album. According to Boziwick, "Julius Mattfeld's reference work *Variety Music Cavalcade* allows us to determine that out of the

---

[9] Dickinson's Herbarium is housed at Harvard's Houghton Library and available through their digital archives; see https://nrs.harvard.edu/urn-3:FHCL.HOUGH:883158.

[10] Dickinson's Music Book (EDR 469) is also available through Harvard's digital archives; see https://iiif.lib.harvard.edu/manifests/view/drs:46653089$1i.

twenty-three most popular pieces of 1843 and 1844, more than half are represented in Dickinson's binders' volume" (84).

"Containing just over one hundred pieces," the book was somewhat unusual for its time, being "more than twice the size of the average binder" (84). It was common nineteenth-century practice for albums to represent a relatively even mix of instrumental and vocal works, as this would have demonstrated a credible level of musical awareness, proficiency, and stylistic acumen. "Vocal music (which was more common to binders' volumes) offered a public display of talent, whereas the more difficult instrumental music was viewed as a demonstration of a more privately refined musical taste" (84). Dickinson's book "is primarily instrumental rather than vocal" (84). Dickinson's considered (and very personal) selection of music seems to support the view that "instrumental music" is "more privately refined" (84). While she did receive training in singing and was afforded opportunities to implement this knowledge (particularly in collaborative settings), singing nevertheless played a very specific role. Her Calvinist upbringing promoted a certain sense of decorum, humility, and private restraint and conduct, and the more public nature of singing practice (notwithstanding sacred activity) was to be avoided where possible. However, instrumental practice and performance (particularly within the domestic space) reflected a more rarefied, tasteful relationship to music as an art form. It is, therefore, not surprising that the majority of Dickinson's music book scores were of an instrumental nature, with almost three-quarters of the album devoted to solo piano music.

As the role of the piano within the home altered throughout the early part of the nineteenth century, so too did the way in which piano music was arranged and published. Due to the rise of the private salon and the move to generate music-making within more diverse and informal settings, composers and arrangers quickly responded by generating material that could be more readily reproduced, while retaining a sense of drama and ceremony found in more formal performance platforms. The piano became the primary source of entertainment, and through this many other forms of artistic language were conveyed. Literature (via hymns, folk and parlor songs, and sentimental ballads), dance (through instrumental versions of common forms such as marches, quicksteps, polkas, and waltzes), and larger-scale works (such as examples of symphonic and operatic variation and transcription) provided a rich menu from which to choose when entertaining both family and guests. Capitalizing on the growth and interest in piano repertoire and practice, and in accordance with her own training, Dickinson sought repertoire that highlights a breadth of interest and knowledge in the instrument's scope and capacity for communication. Some 32 waltzes, transcribed for solo piano, feature in her folio, thereby supporting the notion that she was conversant in popular dance forms of the day. Some of these were (erroneously) attributed to Beethoven, a publishing strategy to actively garner economic gain from the public's interest in European art and music at that time. Examples are evident of a piano duet (Kreutzer's "Overture to Lodoiska"[11]) and solos that demonstrate a particular alacrity for advanced interpretation and virtuoso-esque presentation, such as "The Much Admired Sliding Waltz"[12] and the solo piano suite "L'Enfer Quadrille Diabolique."[13]

In complement to this breadth of piano repertoire is the equally telling inclusion of vocal material. It is here that we see the true influence of external musical idiom. Examples range from Scottish, Irish, and English folk repertoire (such as "Bonny Doon,"[14] "The Lament of the Irish Emigrant,"[15] and "The Rose of Allandale"[16]), to patriotic songs (such as "The Bonnie Clay Flag,"[17] "The Old Granite State,"[18] and "There's a Good Time Coming"[19]), to sentimental ballads (such as "The Old Arm Chair,"[20] "Home, Sweet Home,"[21] and "The Charming Woman"[22]). This range of vocal genre and the diversity of context and narrative position Dickinson's considered selections as a rare and valuable example of her ability to find connection across a diverse lingual paradigm. While it is unclear as to whether Dickinson selected her repertoire based on popularity, diversity (in musical scope and ethnicity), technical challenge, sentimental notion, or all of the above, what is perhaps most intriguing is the way in which she directly engaged these choices and how this process resonated (and arguably informed) her approach to curation, annotation, and amendment within adjunct artistic practice.

While Emily Dickinson clearly did not engage with her chosen repertoire from the perspective of an industry professional, she did leave evidence of editorial and annotative markings within many of the scores that offer a valuable insight regarding her approach to music investigation, rehearsal, and preparation. The

---

[11] The index to Dickinson's music book divides the works into "Duett" [sic], "Variations," "Marches," "Quicksteps," "Waltzes," and "Songs"; for Kreutzer's "Overture to Lodoiska," see seq. 15-28 in the Harvard online manuscript.
[12] See seq. 301-302.
[13] See seq. 325-334.
[14] See seq. 75-78.
[15] See seq. 379-388.
[16] See seq. 421-424.
[17] See seq. 445-448.
[18] See seq. 389-400.
[19] See seq. 425-430.
[20] See seq. 371-378.
[21] See seq. 415-416.
[22] See seq. 435-438.

most critical markings on Dickinson's scores are those pertaining to technique and interpretation. Issues of fingering, tempi, articulation, and nuance (particular dynamic variance and control) attest to her analytical approach during her music practice. This is primarily evident in the piano scores, which support the notion that this repertoire commanded her attention above those of a more vocal nature. The markings, often written in haste and with a degree of urgency, offer an insight into the way in which she edited with the goal of eventual attainment: actively seeking alternative solutions to enable her musical language to be more elegantly and directly constructed and conveyed.

When considering the notion of pianistic process as a form of linguistic analysis, a key component will inevitably be the successful attainment of suitable fingering. An ideal fingering depends on many factors: style, technical requirement, level of technical development, embedded somatic gesture within the composition, and, of course, the size, shape, and facility of the hand. Yet the discovery of the "correct" fingering, one that comfortably fits like a key and its corresponding lock, is imperative in decoding the many complexities when preparing a piece of piano music. Dickinson's marking represents a "laboratory-style" approach to fingering algorithm and arguably suggests a potential annotative schema that permeated into her literary process.

One of the most meaningful examples of fingering annotation is her use of + to denote the thumb. Nineteenth-century published piano music followed two separate models of fingering system: the English and the Continental fingering system.

English System	+ = thumb	1 = index	2 = middle	3 = ring	4 = pinkie
Continental System	1 = thumb	2 = index	3 = middle	4 = ring	5 = pinkie

The English system drew on idiomatic practice predating J. S. Bach's treatise regarding innovative fingering for the harpsichord. Keyboard music prior to this period rarely used the thumb. Bach's reworkings—promoting the crossing of fingers, and a more extensive use of the thumb in extended passage work—redefined the way in which keyboard players approached the preparation of the score. Both systems were in use at the time of Dickinson's musical development, although the English version gradually became obsolete, whereas the Continental version remains as the most widely used point of reference. We find evidence of both systems (in printed form) throughout her album and even her own use of both systems via her bespoke annotations. (See Figures 2.1 and 2.2.)

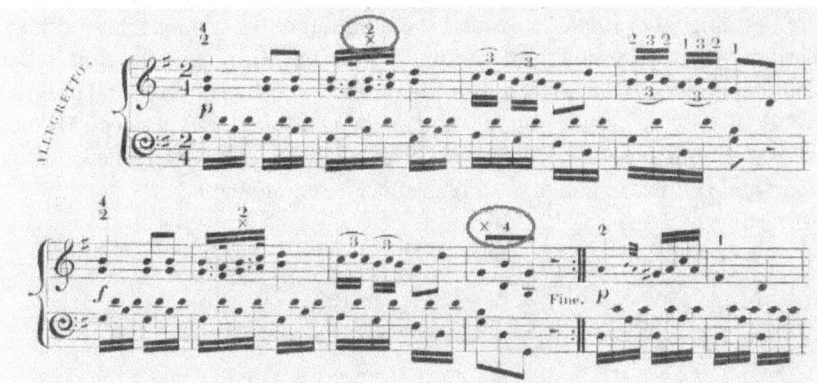

Figure 2.1 EDR 469. Houghton Library, Harvard University. "Di Tanti Palpiti" with variations, Edward L. White – Bars 1-10; see seq. 57, page 1.

Figure 2.2 EDR 469. Houghton Library, Harvard University. Kreutzer's "Overture to Lodoiska," arr. By Charles Czerny (piano duet) – Secondo, Bars 18-32; see seq. 18, page 4.

Emily Dickinson's choice to ascribe an X (+ derivative), primarily as a substitute for the thumb but also as an alternative for adjacent fingerings, provided her with the necessary notation to explore potentially different solutions during her creative process. In this sense, we experience her courage at seeking creative freedom and are afforded a clear connection to similar tropes in the myriad workings and drafts of her poems. These can be best evidenced in her envelope poem manuscripts, of which "We talked with each other about each other" (Fr1506) serves as an example. (See Figure 2.3.) In the process of capturing momentary inspiration, Dickinson was also committed to finding the best lingual example to express the emotion of the moment in question. Can this not also be said for her intimate workings with musical score? In the daily, repetitive cycle of pianistic endeavor, she was called upon to find optimal solutions to often cryptic conundrum; so too was her literary process. The act of conception, adaptation/edit, and "birth" was a sequence that she knew by heart and craftily fashioned to suit her specific requirements.

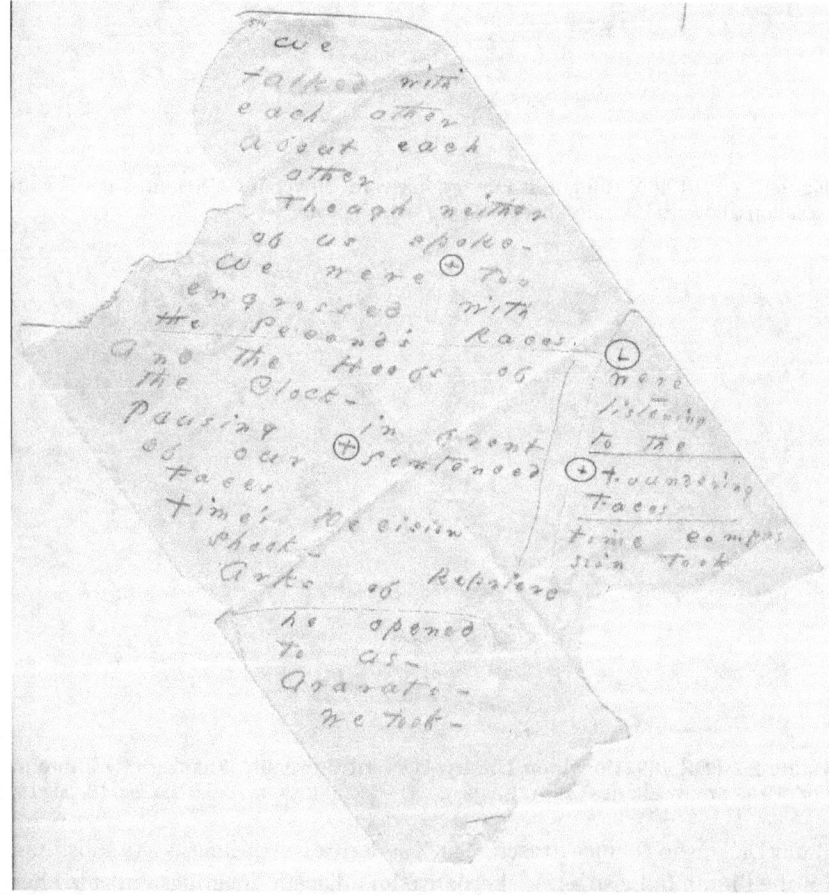

Figure 2.3 "We talked with each other about each other," in Emily Dickinson Collection, Box 6, Folder 52, Amherst College Archives and Special Collections, Amherst College Library

The art of curation and compilation were areas in which Emily Dickinson excelled. Across the broad sweep of her creative enterprise we see commonalities in relation to balance, measurement, proportion, gradient, complement, color, and scope. Her Herbarium exemplifies her relationship to the "language of flowers": hidden messages and metaphoric codes within flora, often sent as gifts to family and friends. Dickinson sought to find order, balance, and symmetry in the construction of her Herbarium. With similar attention to detail, she painstakingly compiled her poems and fascicles and judiciously collated the various musical scores to create her preferred musical catalogue. In seeking out the inherent synchronicity and benefits of employing the language of music, Emily Dickinson functioned as a polylinguist with surprising ease. According to T. W. Higginson's 1870 letter to his wife, Dickinson described reading poetry thusly: "'If I read a book [and] it makes my whole body so cold no fire ever can warm me I know *that* is poetry" (L342a). Similarly, a late poem written on a scrap of stationery opens: "The fascinating chill that Music leaves / Is Earth's corroboration / Of Ecstasy's impediment" (Fr1511). It is clear that both art forms initiated a profound, ecstatic, and visceral response. Extending beyond her utilitarian lingual needs was a desire to express the inexpressible. In music she found a dynamic conduit and a poetic comrade.

"In adequate Music there is a Major and a Minor"

As a natural by-product of her musical training, Emily Dickinson not only retained the fundamental language of music but arguably used it to her advantage. Through strategic implementation, she not only demonstrated her ability to merge the two art forms of poetry and music (for the purpose of a more heightened, linear expression) but, as a direct result, positioned the language of music as a critical tool for expressing areas of emotion that words cannot access. When engaging with the study and practice of music, one inevitably learns the required terminology as a means to access a more wholistic engagement with the creative material on offer. A broadening of knowledge in relation to terms and directions enables the practicing musician to infuse her sound-world with more color, depth, contrast, and therefore greater emotional specificity. During the many hours spent at the piano and through her vocal activities, Emily Dickinson was required to not only engage with musical terminology but, perhaps more importantly, understand how to then put these *linguistic tools* into practice. The act of translating musical terminology/text into sonic equivalence provided a valuable opportunity to then consider the ways in which these musical terms could be adopted within her own literary craft. Dickinson understood the power of this device, as evidenced in many of her poems. What is of special interest is how Dickinson demonstrated this breadth and depth of musical reference and terminology via specific context and setting. This use was always judicious, always apt. Many poems feature a hint of reference, while some focus on a number of musical terms within one setting. What is clear is that, regardless of balance or ratio, Dickinson brings the power of the language of music into focus and, in doing so, promotes polyglottal practice.

While Emily Dickinson solely trained in voice and piano, she was nevertheless aware of the sonic and elemental properties of other instruments. Her exposure to alternative sound-worlds would have primarily occurred through literary translation (i.e., descriptions via books or articles) and through music-based activity within her local community. Elements such as tessitura, tonal quality, and articulative characteristics all played a part in the way that she positioned instruments to speak beyond their immediate domain and purpose. The primary function of the musical instrument was a metaphor. With a sole instrument, she could evoke an enhanced account of a particular emotional need, context, or dilemma. In this sense, she prized the notion of economic delivery with impact. Her use of instruments was very much aligned with an act of representation: the drum as a symbol of personal distress or death; the bugle (or wider brass) as a sign of danger or foreboding; the flute as a metaphor for birdsong and the human voice; the piano as a representative of collective sonic iteration (due to its harmonic, melodic, and articulative capacity); the organ as a symbol of religious "heft" and formality; the violin as the voice of the individual and beauty; and the lute (apropos Shakespearian semantics) as a transporter of love, desire, and ecstasy, a symbolic representation of the ethereal magnetism and power of music.

In the final stanza of her poem "Like Some Old fashioned Miracle –" (Fr408A), Dickinson's speaker refers to "Summer's Recollection" as a "Strain," as memories that replay as melody. Mention of collective instrumentation ("Orchestra") sits in direct juxtaposition to that of the sole "Violin." In this sense, the poet uses musical instruments as a scoping agent: determining size, magnitude, and import. In the end, the "Violin" is put away (replaced), the individual's voice is silenced, and the poem closes with "And Ear, and Heaven – numb –." The silence, so to speak, is deafening. In contrast, the sounds of nature in "I dreaded that first Robin, so," (Fr347) are powerful and frightening. The poem describes an intimate account of personal struggle. Although the Robin is now "mastered," the speaker recalls once feeling that if only she could live until the first sounds of spring had passed, she would be well, with "all Pianos in the Woods" no longer having the "power to mangle me." Here, the poet uses the piano as a direct reference to the song, or "voice," of birds. Capable of various pitches, with a wide register, the piano provides harmonic, textural, and tonal contrast. The image in the poem is that of "a vast number of birds, all singing at the same time and singing at various levels or pitches" (Reglin 94).

The opening of "Put up my lute!" (Fr324) reads as a declamatory act. Here, "Music" can be read as a metaphor for poetic practice and the lute as its conduit and portal of release. There is a sense that the speaker's "Music" is falling on deaf ears (or ear, rather, since the speaker states there is a "sole ear" she "cared to charm"): a stony, "Passive" response circulates above and around her work, while never fully accepting or receiving it. Neither emotional entreaty nor religious (moral) piety will engender a response. To "awaken" her listeners/readers, the speaker wonders whether "the 'Memnon' of the Desert" could "Teach" her. In *Emily Dickinson's Poems: As She Preserved Them*, Cristanne Miller notes that "Memnon" refers to the "huge ruined statues in Egypt at the entrance gate of a mortuary temple. After the northern colossus was damaged (27 BCE), it produced a strange musical sound at sunrise. Early Greek and Roman tourists named the statue Memnon after a Trojan hero who sang to his mother at dawn" (752 n138). The speaker understands the power of music/poetry but does not know how to harness it.

Although Dickinson refers to the drum in only five of her poems, the drum serves as a channel for articulating the ceremony and profundity of human struggle and loss. For example, in the poem "My Triumph lasted till the Drums" (Fr1212), the speaker questions the validity and cost of victory. The "delusive image of victory only makes worse the pain of defeat. But Dickinson is equally disturbed and dissatisfied by victory when it is achieved" (Wolosky 113). Here, the drum symbolizes the point at which the speaker's "Triumph" is no longer viable: a musical reference denoting demarcation, announcement, and prophesy. In the poem, "the Drums / Had left the Dead alone" and the speaker "stole along / To where the finished Faces / Conclusion turned on me / And then I hated Glory." Shira Wolosky reads this poem as a war poem in which Dickinson is imagining "herself walking among scraps of body" (113), or the "finished Faces," which are the cost of war, regardless of which side was victorious.

The drum also features significantly in "I felt a Funeral, in my Brain" (Fr340), one of Dickinson's best-known poems. The poet captures, with alarming clarity and intensity, the process of mental decline. She vividly describes the process of separation between mind and body. It is in the second stanza that we experience true sonic impact. She knew, and intrinsically felt, the metaphoric qualities of the drum. In inescapable reference to its links with war (particularly her own experience regarding the military-related sound-world of the Civil War) and therefore a heralding of potential destruction and death, her use of the drum signals a sense of mental deterioration—an annihilation of the true, interior self. The incessant "beating – beating," repetitive and inescapable, is bare and primal; it is without melody and therefore without individual voice, causing the speaker to feel as though her "mind was going numb –."

The third and fourth stanzas explore another sound-world that Dickinson would have been familiar with: bells. Bells, as a provocative metaphor, feature in 28 poems. Her religious activity throughout her formative years and the close proximity between the Dickinson family home and their church offered the poet a significant opportunity to observe their sound *aurally*—timbre, quality, tempo, and duration. She would have also intrinsically understood their role, particularly in relation to death, which was rife in 1862, the date R. W. Franklin gives as the most likely date of composition for the poem. The speaker feels "Boots of Lead" in her "Soul" and then hears "Space" "toll, / As all the Heavens were a Bell, / And Being, but an Ear, . . . then a Plank in Reason, broke, . . . And hit a World, at every plunge, / And Finished knowing – then –." Barton Levi St. Armand summarizes these two instrumental metaphors and illuminates Dickinson's ability to access a full range of musical language for her specific needs and to produce specific effects: "The drums of a wartime funeral service merge with the tolling bells of simple village rites to produce a surreal cacophony, a Dead March that grates upon the very soul. External and internal death are merged" (108). Though the poem's speaker "Finished knowing," the reader is left with an "ambiguity that obscures meaning" (108). However, it is an ambiguity filled with sound and feeling and a haunting beauty that one does not easily forget.

An oft-cited poem when addressing musical reference in Dickinson's work is "Musicians wrestle everywhere –" (Fr229B). Here we find a speaker in a heightened sensory state who is attuned to sonic language beyond immediate, everyday sounds: people in conversation, birdsong, church hymns. The first stanza, which introduces the cast of celestial "Musicians"—performers of the divine music of "the Spheres"—struggling against earthly sonic congestion, is an evocative one. Her use of the term "silver strife" describes the ethereal quality of a sound that is hard to define, difficult to categorize, and riddled with conflict.

The second stanza features a number of musical and instrumental references, adding color, timbre, and pace. Her reference to "Band" dressed in "brass and scarlet" speaks to the look of many marching and military bands that were a feature of Amherst during her lifetime. The "Tamborin" (the term for either an old French drum or a historic, lively Provençal dance in duple meter) and the "Hymn" denote her breadth of knowledge in both the sound and origin of musical instruments and forms. Her use of the term "Treble" suggests the sound of the heavenly feminine: light, high, shimmery, and outwardly delicate. All of these describe what the wrestling "Musicians" are *not*. The sound of "the

Spheres," as "Some – say – it is," is unknowable and indescribable (although that is the aim of the poem); a music we can only "ascertain" after death.

One of the best examples of a poem that is *defined* by the sound, nature, and connotation of the musical instrument is "I've heard an Organ talk, sometimes –" (Fr211). Unlike many other poems which cite music as a feature device, this poem positions the chosen instrument (in this case the organ) as the sole determinant of the speaker's emotional state. The speaker cannot identify the *dialect* of the organ's sound, but the distinct *quality* and *timbre* of its sonic presence leaves an indelible, suspended mark. The speaker hears the organ "talk" "In a Cathedral Aisle" and understands nothing it says, yet she still holds her "breath, the while –." The poem continues to unpack the profound effect of the organ's sound by suggesting that the speaker has been transformed. She has been transported to a "more Bernardine" existence, referencing Bernardine Cistercian nuns, who vow to honor stability, obedience, and conversion of life through prayer and abstinence. But this transformation comes without the speaker ever understanding, although being fully aware of, the organ's power: "[I] knew not what was done to me / In that old Chapel Aisle."

Emily Dickinson's determined use of musical language, and the ways in which she wove and assimilated it with her own literary voice, is equally evident in her use of music terminology. She understood the creative power and distinct benefits when employing musical directive, whether standard or more musically bespoke by nature. A known language, this was the language of her youth, one that she embodied in both practice and theory. One of the best poetic examples of Dickinson's use of music terminology is "Better – than Music!" (Fr378). Here, Dickinson employs a wide range of musical terms and reference as a means of more explicitly revealing the interior, emotional dialogue. The opening two lines reflect the importance that she placed on music (denoted by the use of capitalization and exclamation mark), suggesting that the "better" version of it was a very personal one: "Better – than Music! / For I – who heard it –." The second stanza offers a number of key musical terms that serve to propel her directive, which is to describe the distinction between "This" sound and all other types of music she had known before. Her use of the term "stanza" draws on poetic metric device and her intimate knowledge of hymn construction. The use of "Composer" as an artistic creator and powerful presence is exemplified by her mention of "perfect Mozart." The term "keyless Rhyme" connotes an existing known structure that lacks origin, identity, and security. The final stanza refers to an additional set of terms. Dickinson's use of the word "cadence" alludes not only to a "fall of the voice in reading or speaking," according to Dickinson's *Webster*, but also to "repose; the termination of a harmonical phrase on a repose or on a perfect chord."[23] Further, a musical cadence "may be said to contain the essence of the melodic (including rhythmic) and harmonic movement, hence of the musical language, that characterizes the style to which it belongs" (Rockstro). It is here that the poet creatively articulates a sense of containment, urgency, and value of the "better" music. Her use of the term "Humming," the "buzz" "of a bee" or to "blend sounds in a low, murmuring noise," according to the *Emily Dickinson Lexicon*,[24] evokes a sonic utterance without definition or clear identity. "Rehearsal" in the penultimate line infers issues of draft, practice, and preparatory practice before the final act of returning home: "Humming – until my faint Rehearsal – / Drop into tune – around the Throne –."

In her poem "Dying at my music!" (Fr1003), Dickinson begins by using the term "music" as a personal descriptor—that of her own creative language. This reference also suggests that she viewed her poetic practice as one of musical construction: with harmonic and melodic sensibilities. The use of "Bubble! Bubble!" suggests sonic onomatopoeia, the act of simmering yet disguised internal emotional dialogue: "Dying at my music! / Bubble! Bubble!" In the next line, her reference to "the Octave's run," denoting both a poetic and musical device (a stanza or set of eight lines or notes, respectively), articulates issues of length, duration, and spatial design. The use of "Ritardando," a gradual reduction in speed, works in direct opposition to her idea of "Burst the Windows" in line four, which suggests more sudden, urgent, even spontaneous movement. The burst is followed by the gradual reduction in speed, leaving only "Phials . . . and the Sun!" The speaker's musical/poetic output has so strained her that she feels as empty as "Phials," or vials, which, according to the *Lexicon*, could be thought of as "empty receptacle[s]" as well as a "physical frame from which the spirit has departed."

Emily Dickinson's affinity with the language of music is never more present than in her use of music as a metaphor. Throughout her entire literary canon, she returns to musical imagery and allusion as a preferred means of self-expression, critical reflection, and inspired articulation. Music became a symbol of the deepest aspects of her primary themes: death, spirituality, nature, love, and the quest for true connection with the authentic self. In her poem "There's a certain Slant of light" (Fr320), for example, Dickinson highlights a sense of depression, weight, even impending death via a compelling connection of light, time, and sound. She closely observes the quality of afternoon light during the winter months—light that is low-level,

---

[23] See http://edl.byu.edu/webster/term/2384081.

[24] See http://edl.byu.edu/lexicon/term/560787.

indistinct, and fleeting. Although limited, it carries weight and moves by increment. Her sense of its oppression is fashioned by the metaphoric use of religious music, or "Cathedral Tunes." The use of capitalization highlights the music's somber, heavy, and traditional (arguably patriarchal) quality. Dickinson employs the musical to define and depict the literal: a "light" that "oppresses" with such power that it causes "internal difference" and even "the Landscape listens –."

"He fumbles at your Soul" (Fr477B) finds the poet at her most awe-struck and arguably her most damning. According to Adrienne Rich, this "poem has intimations of both seduction and rape merged with the intense force of a religious experience" (105). It is an example of a poem "about the poet's relationship to her own power, which is exteriorized in masculine form, much as masculine poets have invoked the female Muse" (105). Dickinson describes an outside force that is male, penetrating, and all-encompassing, with the piano as self. The act of fumbling, like "Players at the Keys," suggests a form of warm-up or rehearsal, as when a player (the pianist or God-like male figure) plays a scale or a small passage to correctly orient himself in relation to the touch, weight, quality, and dimensions of the keyboard. Once this has been achieved, the "full Music" begins—a rendering of playing her soul with full force, ultimate control, and tantalizing gesture. As the performance continues, the piano is stunned; as each note, each phrase is stroked and pulled from the body of the piano's soul, the metaphoric self is incrementally broken down. She continues to use musical imagery to paint a further state of slow and steady annihilation. The use of the term "brittle" alludes to an articulative musical quality, akin to *staccato*, which is defined by its detached timbre. One of the pianist's most powerful strategies is that of seductive control of tempo. Achieved through a micro-controlled level of touch and voicing, the musical impact can be one of instant transformation or sustained release. The "Hammers" become "fainter" and "slow" until there is an "imperial Thunderbolt – / That peels your naked soul –."

The myth of Orpheus provides the backdrop for Emily Dickinson's poem "Bind me – I still can sing –" (Fr1005), and Dickinson strategically weaves musical reference to create meaning and context. Orpheus was a Greek hero blessed with supernatural musical powers who could sing and play so beautifully that animals, trees, and rocks were united in dance. Bound and banished, he was torn to pieces by Thracian Maenads, after which his head and his signature lyre were thrown into the river Hebrus and then floated to Lesbos. It is claimed that his severed head continued to sing. With astounding economy, Emily Dickinson uses the human voice as a fitting metaphor for the poetic. Despite adversity—attempts to "Bind" and "Banish" her—the poet is determined to be heard. Orpheus's lyre becomes a "mandolin" in the poem, and the poet's voice continues to sing as it rises "to Paradise."

In "There came a Wind like a Bugle –" (Fr1618), the strident, cutting sound of the bugle depicts the bare, elemental, exposed quality of nature. The poem vividly paints the awe-inspiring, fundamental power of nature: an unpredictable force that has the capacity to override human control and rationale. While many of Emily Dickinson's poems address the more benevolent aspects of nature, this poem speaks of the polar opposite— "Electric" energy, anticipation, trepidation, and destruction. The bugle, a "hunting horn" or "a military instrument of music," according to Dickinson's *Webster*,[25] serves as an ideal simile: its piercing sound normally associated with death (in the hunt or in battle) here heralds a natural phenomenon—a wind that has the power to wreak havoc and obliterate.

In "Split the Lark – and you'll find the Music –" (Fr905), the poet explores the tension between empirical knowledge and felt truth. Opening with a direct challenge, the poem demands the reader, if skeptical of the origin of creative impetus ("Music"), to "Split" the bird open to assuage any doubt. The poem's message: the desire to forage and dissect creativity, while understandable, is bloody and messy and unnecessarily destructive of the bird's/poet's inherent craft. The lark, a bird associated with the morning sun and "rapturous and soaring flight" (Baker 70), *is* the poet: the lark's song is the poet's literary voice. The dissection reveals "Bulb after Bulb,"[26] from which stems a "Silver" stream of spontaneous, creative testimony. The "Lutes be old" and cannot compete with the beauty of the bird's song: such quality can only surpass the lute's more standard melodic voice. The poem ends by questioning the reader: "Now, do you doubt that your Bird was true?" The lark in Dickinson's poem stands as a symbol of individuality (the lark's song "resembles that of no other bird") and something felt, rather than understood (Baker 70).

In keeping with the theme of music as a metaphor for scale and space, the poem "The Birds begun at Four o'clock –" (Fr504B) opens with Emily Dickinson's homage to the sound of nature at dawn. Here, the poet draws on the cacophony of birdsong at this time of day, individual voices that obey no particular design, order, or restraint in their delivery. Their "Music" is prolific and driven by "independent Extasy," with no need for specific attention or recognition. The event is regular and welcome, but there are few "Witnesses"—an "Occasional Man" and, of course, the poet, who records the event, perhaps because the

---

[25] See http://edl.byu.edu/webster/term/2339835.

[26] According to the *Lexicon*, "bulb" could refer to a "vital organ" or "essential body part" as well as "note," "tune," or "melody"; see http://edl.byu.edu/lexicon/term/617973.

birdsong has faded "By Six" and "The Miracle that introduced" the "Day" is "Forgotten" until tomorrow.

Similarly, in her poem "Further in Summer than the Birds –" (Fr895A), Emily Dickinson scans a wider view of the earth's lyric beauty:

> Emily expresses her keen awareness of the many keys in which earth's melody is played . . . the song of birds, the murmuring of bees, bells, and the voice of the wind. . . . the shrill singing of an axe in the woods, the bleating of sheep, thunder, the pounding of horses' hooves, the ticking of clocks, the brook's laugh, the elegy of the cricket's voice. No sound is too small or too large to escape the poet's appreciative attention. (McNaughton 22–23)

Building on Keats's sentiment in his sonnet "The Grasshopper and the Cricket," Dickinson penned "her own elegy for the poetry of earth" (Loeffelholz 145). However, "unlike Keats's cricket by the hearth, Dickinson's cricket does not sing of nature's persistence within culture but of a natural death that culture cannot repair" (Jackson 77). In the sixth stanza, Dickinson uses musical key as a metaphor for home, place, and identity. Melody (or lack thereof) is superseded, replaced by an earthly music that is both infinite and mesmerizing: "The Earth has many keys – / Where Melody is not / Is the Unknown Peninsula – / Beauty – is Nature's Fact –."

In the poem "I think I was enchanted" (Fr627), Dickinson continues to employ the language of music to elucidate emotional premise. In this salute to Elizabeth Barrett Browning, Dickinson codifies the nineteenth-century female poet, fashioning a transcendental metaphor via the study of the size, shape, and sound of nature. Through Dickinson's perceptive lens, the most ordinary "Tunes" in nature become a full-scale, interdisciplinary art form: a "Titanic Opera." In this sense, music and nature-as-metaphor become an allegory for the poet's own literary position: a female poet with the power to make the "Dark" feel "beautiful."

While there are clearly many poems that serve to advocate the notion that Emily Dickinson *thought* musically, the following poem seems to expertly encapsulate the essence of her poetic manifesto. In "This World is not conclusion" (Fr373), Dickinson stands facing the interface between human consciousness and infinity. Despite our "Philosophy" and "Sagacity," a "Species stands beyond" that we cannot comprehend. Her reference to (and differentiation of) "Music" and "Sound" is an important one. Music connotes the "Invisible": the ethereal, the creative genius that is eternally tacit. However, Dickinson also concedes to the earthly presence of "positive, as Sound." Through the language of music, Dickinson finds her perfect setting and her master trope: "It beckons" and "baffles" and "Strong Hallelujahs roll" as a "Tooth" "nibbles at the soul –." As Emily Dickinson embraced the possibility of an individualized musical language by linguistically segueing between literary and musical vernacular, she also systematically sought a personal paradigm in which to produce her own brand of music—one built on her own terms.

"I can improvise better at night" – Emily Dickinson's "riffs"

Emily Dickinson, in her quest for personal creative control and emancipation, judiciously explored the possibilities of artistic innovation within prescribed boundary. Her life coincided with a period in American history that, in musical terms, would alter the way in which we view music: as a mirror for human growth, freedom, and democracy. This revolution provided a means of liberation and a "tool for personal expression beyond what the original composer may have had in mind" (Hasse 57). Her quest for emotional release, within constrained frameworks, resonated with the social and political climate of the time. As she quietly determined a path of private creative enterprise, free from the confines of tradition and expectation, she drew on the practice and idiomatic flexibility of music.

While Dickinson was not directly trained in the popular, pre-jazz music of the day, she was aware of it: "The presence of at least three minstrel tunes in Dickinson's binder and her accounts of visiting the servants, or of Charles Thompson[27] leading her reading club in a dance, demonstrates that this type of music was in the air, performed from the oral tradition as well as from published piano editions for parlor entertainment, or fiddlers' tune books for social dancing" (Boziwick 94). The minstrel music offers contemporary readers a valuable opportunity to observe from where she may have gleaned certain jazz techniques and idiomatic gestures. These pieces, in combination with written accounts of her conversations (a sharing of musical ideas and repertoire) with servants, helped inform and shape her piano improvisations and her literary craftsmanship. There have been very few substantiated records confirming Emily Dickinson's improvisatory skills, such as her saying to John Graves, "I can improvise better at night" (Sewall 406). However, what does exist remains important in terms of accurately describing her approach and method and, in some cases, the recipient's subsequent reflection. Clara Newman Turner, for example, recalled "that before seating herself at the piano Emily covered the upper and lower octaves so that the length of the keyboard might correspond to that of the old-fashioned instrument on which she had learned to play" (Sewall 406 n4). This description paints a picture of a young woman

---

[27] Charles Thompson was "an African American man who for decades was a janitor for Amherst College and laborer for the Dickinsons" (Boziwick 94).

who felt at home at the keyboard, with a certain level of confidence in the requisite techniques and mannerisms. They would have been standard fodder for any pianist to then be able to tackle the more complex act of improvisation. Kate Anthon recalled Dickinson's invented melodies "in a letter to Martha Bianchi, October 8, 1917, . . . those 'blissful evenings at Austin's' (in the late 1850s) when Emily was 'often at the piano playing weird & beautiful melodies, all from her own inspiration'" (Sewall 406 n4). Dickinson's youthful, engaging, and enigmatic spirit instilled fun, spontaneity, mischief, and creative zeal. George Boziwick, for example, records a passage from MacGregor Jenkins's memoir titled *Emily Dickinson Friend and Neighbor* that highlights the playfulness and humor of Dickinson's personality, which extended to her musical approach and composition: "[S]he would fly to the piano, if the mood required, and thunder out a composition of her own which she laughingly but appropriately called 'The Devil'" (93). Dickinson's forays in improvised performance may have been all too rare and arguably fleeting, but her need to improvise extended far beyond external acclaim. Most of her music improvisation was carried out alone and at night. In this sense, she strategically carved a nocturnal platform for her creative experiments, one where music and poetry were not only equally welcome but born from a common source.

It is not difficult to agree that Emily Dickinson, as polyglot, actively sought to work in a way that maximized her ability to create art on her own terms and within her own designated boundaries. Whether seated at the piano or her writing desk, Dickinson dared to experiment with rhythm, tempo, space, and tone in real time and in doing so expertly transferred her improvised "riffs" through her pen and paper. Camille Paglia positions the poet as an expert improviser: "Singsong rhythms and neat rhymes are always spurious in Dickinson, the first modernist master of syncopation and atonality" (638). Paul Crumbley takes Paglia's assertions one step further. Crumbley directly connects Dickinson's rhythmic experiments with those of the modern jazz musician, with a particular focus on the ways in which she innovated within traditional forms and constructs: "Though she frequently employs common ballad meter . . . her poetry is in no way constrained by that form; rather, she performs like a jazz artist who uses rhythm and meter to revolutionize readers' perceptions of those structures" (248). One of the most interesting aspects of this study is the comparative use of creative "cell." In sympathy with the process of construction during jazz improvisation, Emily Dickinson painstakingly crafted her poetry based on cellular patterns. It is perhaps in her idiosyncratic use of the "cell"—a nucleus of thought that transcends scope yet also promotes the pithy—that her genius resides. When the true heart of the work is built on small fragments of sound (or text), the possibility for loose interpretation, translation, and presentation is significantly reduced; issues of accuracy become paramount. Paul Balmer, in his book *Stéphane Grappelli: A Life in Jazz*, speaks of Yehudi

Menuhin's recollections of working with Grappelli. In particular, Balmer provides a selection of Menuhin's insights regarding key elements of standard jazz practice: "Yehudi discovered that jazz, in common with many other improvised music, is very much more difficult to bluff. He felt that, in order to give life to music, 'you have to be trained in that way, to follow the germ, the cell—the rhythmic cell, the melodic cell, the harmonic cell—as it unfolds'" (79). Balmer then extends this discussion by outlining Menuhin's response to the jazz musician's true mission—an inventory of the critical components that serve as a gateway to the musician's navigation: "Yehudi realised that the jazz musician had to know the *music*—not the notation, that inadequate map, but the melody and how it flowed, the harmony and what it implied and the rhythm and how it developed" (79).

But what of the jazz musician who seeks out Dickinson's texts? Are these texts easily accessible? Does the artist choose to synchronize his or her own musical style with the inherent improvisatory qualities of her work? Is Emily Dickinson's writing "jazz friendly"? The 2017 jazz album *Wild Lines: Improvising Emily Dickinson*, devised, curated, and performed by the American saxophonist Jane Ira Bloom, successfully tackles these questions. Bloom first became fascinated with Dickinson's literary canon in 2009, after hearing a lecture by Alice Quinn and a presentation by George Boziwick in New York City. Bloom was particularly interested in Boziwick's session, as it was here that she was first introduced to Emily Dickinson's music improvisations. After further reading, Bloom became fascinated with Dickinson's envelope poems and the ways in which she used fragments of creative material to construct her poems and, in some cases, letters. In an interview with National Sawdust Log, Bloom explains that it was the combination of Dickinson's personas—musician and mosaicist—that inspired her to start the project:

> I was inspired by Emily Dickinson because she was a piano player and an improviser. Any time I read her poetry, it felt musical to me—and it felt improvisatory. It freed me from a traditional approach, which would have been writing a tone poem, or setting her poems to music. I used fragments that sparked my imagination—that made something light up inside of me—to inspire the music. It's a much more abstract relationship to the text than a specific rendering or an underscoring of her words. (Pellegrinelli)

As Bloom progressed through the initial stages of the process of preparing the album, she became increasingly aware of the tension derived from Emily Dickinson's dutiful "performances," in differing roles. The poet's ability to adapt, "busk," mold, and weave her artistic material resonates with similar traits and expectations of the practicing jazz musician. Bloom was particularly interested in the *musicality* of Dickinson's writing and its role in the process of creating the texts and the attraction of its elusive power:

> In my mind, she was a jazz musician. She did what jazz musicians do. When I listen to her poetry, I feel like I'm listening to Thelonious Monk. . . . There is a rhythm [in her poetry] that must appeal to the musical mind, and a musical mind must have had a part in making it. (Pellegrinelli)

Bloom continues to explore common themes (such as metaphor) in both Emily Dickinson's writing and improvisatory practice:

> Isn't that the power of the poetic metaphor? Jazz musicians do this all the time; something from one place and something from a completely different place merge. Together they create something powerful. That's what so much of her language does for me. (Pellegrinelli)

Acknowledging the palpable constraints under which Dickinson lived and worked, it is perhaps unsurprising that the act of improvisation served as a meaningful conduit for her artistic and personal imperatives. The elemental nature and methodology of the improvisatory act closely mirrored that of her own literary process, particularly in the strategic exercise and manipulation of the "miniature" to create a colossus of thought and feeling. Her eclectic reimagining of *ostinato* phraseology while meticulously maintaining her solo "voice" denotes a "riff" master, a product of her place yet ahead of her time.

Emily Dickinson actively sought a creative mandate that could fuel her inner desires, showcase her skills and talents, and nurture her imagination, while concurrently claiming the freedom to do so on her own terms. Her friends and family commented on her connection to and natural affinity with music, and her musical activity was by no means exclusively private. In many ways, the origin of her musical experience was neither straightforward nor simple. Yet despite the inevitable caveats that came with this experience—religion, class, and gender—Dickinson successfully manifested a way in which music could work *for* her. The opportunity to train, practice, and immerse herself in the language of music provided Dickinson with the incentive to implement music as a viable and radical tool in her idiosyncratic acts of storytelling.

The poet's act of incorporating the language of music into her everyday life and artistic practice was, conceivably, more straightforward than first imagined. Her knowledge of the scope, structure, and philosophical purpose of music endures through her very personal act of transference and translation. Music pervaded her poems and letters, as a metaphor, directive, allusion, and as a vivid and radical imagistic device. Music informed the ways in which she conceived and curated her work, providing sonic navigation when words proved limited. Music became the one language that Emily Dickinson trusted as an equal partner to her beloved literary *patois*. This creative "marriage" stands as an inescapable heartbeat throughout her work—a life force that enables the speaker and reader to emotionally connect. Dickinson's "musical" legacy continues through the work of scholars, practitioners, and their respective audiences: the act of setting her literary canon to music; the staging and performance of her work in spoken, sung, and instrumental paradigms; the growth in narration and translation of her life and craft across different media; and the desire for enhanced critical conversation and debate. These efforts serve as an ongoing tool for the preservation and cultivation of her work via a contemporary lens. Her employment of the language of music as a device of choice not only offered release for Dickinson but also paved the way for music scholars and practitioners to engage with her work, in confidence that the common dialect is a shared one. Emily Dickinson's love of music and language, in addition to her quiet dedication to polyglottal practice, became her trusted aide and the inspiration for her private, electric metamorphosis.

Works Cited

The following abbreviations are used to refer to the writings of Emily Dickinson:

Fr *The Poems of Emily Dickinson*, edited by R. W. Franklin, Harvard UP, 1998. Citation by poem number.

L *The Letters of Emily Dickinson*, edited by Thomas H. Johnson and Theodora Ward, Harvard UP, 1958. Citation by letter number.

Amaral, Ana Luísa. "Ms. Difficult: Translating Emily Dickinson." *The Paris Review*, 12 April 2019, www.theparisreview.org/blog/2019/04/12/ms-difficult-translating-emily-dickinson/.
Baker, James V. "The Lark in English Poetry." *Prairie Schooner*, vol. 24, no. 1, Spring 1950, pp. 70–79.
Balmer, Paul. *Stéphane Grappelli: A Life in Jazz*. Bobcat Books, 2008.
Bianchi, Martha Dickinson. *Emily Dickinson Face to Face*. Riverside Press, 1932.
Bingham, Millicent Todd. *Emily Dickinson's Home*. Harper, 1955.
Boziwick, George. "Emily Dickinson's Music Book: A Performative Exploration." *The Emily Dickinson Journal*, vol. 25, no. 1, 2016, pp. 83–105.
Child, Lydia Maria. *The Frugal Housewife*. Carter and Hendee, 1830.
Crumbley, Paul. "Emily Dickinson." *The Oxford Companion to Women's Writing in the United States*, edited by Cathy N. Davidson and Linda Wagner-Martin, Oxford UP, 1995.

Dickinson, Emily. *Emily Dickinson's Poems: As She Preserved Them*, edited by Cristanne Miller, The Belknap Press of Harvard UP, 2016.

----. *Herbarium, circa 1839–1846.* MS Am 1118.11, Houghton Library, Harvard University, https://nrs.harvard.edu/urn-3:FHCL.HOUGH:883158.

----. *[Music]: a bound volume of miscellaneous sheet music, without title page, with Emily Dickinson's autograph [?] on flyleaf, 1844-1852.* Houghton Library, Harvard University, https://iiif.lib.harvard.edu/manifests/view/drs:46653089$1i.

Emily Dickinson Lexicon website, Brigham Young University, 2007, http://edl.byu.edu/index.php.

England, Martha Winburn. *Hymns Unbidden: Donne, Herbert, Blake, Emily Dickinson, and the Hymnographers.* New York Public Library, 1966.

Fuss, Diana. "Interior Chambers: The Emily Dickinson Homestead." *Differences: A Journal of Feminist Cultural Studies*, vol. 10, no. 3, Fall 1998, pp. 1–46.

Hart, Ellen Louise. "Alliteration, Emphasis, and Spatial Prosody in Dickinson's Manuscript Letters." *Reading Emily Dickinson's Letters*, edited by Jane Donahue Eberwein and Cynthia MacKenzie, U of Massachusetts P, 1996, pp. 213–238.

Hasse, John E. and Tad Lathrop. *Discover Jazz.* Pearson, 2011.

Jackson, Virginia. *Dickinson's Misery: A Theory of Lyric Reading.* Princeton UP, 2005.

Leyda, Jay. *The Years and Hours of Emily Dickinson*, vol. 1. Archon, 1970.

Loeffelholz, Mary. *Dickinson and the Boundaries of Feminist Theory.* U of Illinois P, 1991.

Matthews, Cerys. "Poetry and Music Are More Closely Related Than We Think." *The Guardian*, 7 June 2016, https://www.theguardian.com/books/2016/jun/07/cerys-matthews-poetry-and-music-closely-think.

McDowell, Marta. *Emily Dickinson's Gardening Life: The Plants & Places That Inspired the Iconic Poet.* Timber Press, 2019.

McNaughton, Ruth Flanders. "The Imagery of Emily Dickinson." *University of Nebraska Studies*, January 1949.

Miller, Cristanne. *Emily Dickinson: A Poet's Grammar.* Harvard UP, 1987.

----. *Reading in Time: Emily Dickinson in the Nineteenth Century.* U of Massachusetts P, 2012.

Murray, Aife. *Maid as Muse: How Servants Changed Emily Dickinson's Life and Language.* U of Massachusetts P, 2010.

Paglia, Camille. *Sexual Personae: Art and Decadence from Nefertiti to Emily Dickinson.* Yale UP, 1990.

Pellegrinelli, Lara. "Jane Ira Bloom: Exploring the Unruly Music of Emily Dickinson." *National Sawdust Log*, 17 November 2019, https://nationalsawdust.org/thelog/2017/11/14/jane-ira-bloom/.

Phillips, Elizabeth. *Emily Dickinson: Personae and Performance.* Pennsylvania State UP, 1988.

Reglin, Louise Winn. *Music in the Life and Poetry of Emily Dickinson.* U of North Texas, Master's thesis, 1971.

Rich, Adrienne. "Vesuvius at Home: The Power of Emily Dickinson." *Shakespeare's Sisters: Feminist Essays on Women Poets*, edited by Sandra M. Gilbert and Susan Gubar, Indiana UP, 1979, pp. 99–121.

Rockstro, William S., et al. "Cadence." *Grove Music Online*, 20 January 2001, https://doi.org/10.1093/gmo/9781561592630.article.04523.

Sewall, Richard B. *The Life of Emily Dickinson*. Harvard UP, 1994.

Short, Bryan C. "Emily Dickinson and the Origins of Language." *The Emily Dickinson Journal*, vol. 9, no. 2, 2000, pp. 109–119.

Small, Judy Jo. *Positive as Sound: Emily Dickinson's Rhyme*. U of Georgia P, 1990.

St. Armand, Barton Levi. *Emily Dickinson and Her Culture: The Soul's Society*. Cambridge UP, 1984.

Van Loon, Hendrik Willem. "Emily Dickinson and Frederic Chopin." *Van Loon's Lives*. Simon and Schuster, 1942.

Watts, Isaac. *The Psalms, Hymns, and Spiritual Songs of the Rev. Isaac Watts, D.D.*, edited by Samuel M. Worcester, Crocker & Brewster, 1834.

Webster, Noah. *An American Dictionary of the English Language*, 2 vol. reprint of the 1841 edition, Adams Brothers, 1844. Online renovated edition at http://edl.byu.edu/webster.

Whicher, George. *This Was a Poet: A Critical Biography of Emily Dickinson*. Ann Arbor Paperbacks, 1992.

White, Fred. *Approaching Emily Dickinson: Critical Currents and Crosscurrents since 1960*. Camden House, 2008.

Willis, Elizabeth. "Lyric Dissent." *Boundary 2*, vol. 36, no. 3, Fall 2009, pp. 229–234.

Wolosky, Shira. "Public and Private in Dickinson's War Poetry." *A Historical Guide to Emily Dickinson*, edited by Vivian R. Pollak, Oxford UP, 2004.

Chapter 3

The Notorious E.E.D.:
Rap in the Poems of Emily Dickinson

Holly Norton
University of Northwestern Ohio

Abstract

Contemporary readers with only a compulsory introduction to Emily Dickinson and a few of her poems may imagine a woman in white tending flowers, baking cakes, and listening to the buzzing of bees. However, many poems explore themes that we also see in the work of rappers such as the Notorious B.I.G. (Christopher George Latore Wallace) and 2Pac (Tupac Amaru Shakur). The contexts in which Dickinson and these rappers created their art could not be more different—Dickinson's having derived from a position of privilege in the mid-1800s, and Wallace and Shakur having done their work within the context of urban violence and poverty in the late twentieth century. Despite the clear disparities, surprising intersections exist between Dickinson's poetry and rap music, revealing fruitful ways of reading nineteenth-century texts in conjunction with one of today's most influential music (and poetic) genres.

Key words: death, immortality, twentieth-century rap music

***

Contemporary readers with only a compulsory introduction to Emily Dickinson and a few of her poems may imagine a woman in white tending flowers, baking cakes, and listening to the buzzing of bees. However, Dickinson's speakers reveal in many poems the kind of metaphysical confrontation with death that is also found in the work of twentieth-century rappers such as the Notorious B.I.G. (Christopher George Latore Wallace) and 2Pac (Tupac Amaru Shakur). The contexts in which Dickinson and these rappers created their art greatly differed—Dickinson's having derived from a position of privilege in the middle of the nineteenth century, and the Notorious B.I.G. and 2Pac having done their work within the context of urban violence and poverty in the late twentieth century. Although their lives were very different, their explorations of death, the afterlife, and artistic immortality align in fascinating ways.

One central theme in the work of all three—Dickinson, the Notorious B.I.G., and 2Pac—is questioning Christianity. Dickinson as skeptical of traditional church practices is well known. Dickinson refused, for example, "to join the girls at Mount Holyoke who recognized Christ as their Savior," and she never "joined her family's church in Amherst" (Sewall 138). In fact, in her first month at Mount Holyoke seminary, she declared herself a "no hoper," the three choices being those who had already professed a hope in Christ, those who were considering a hope in Christ, and those who did not feel a call (Ackmann 35). Indeed, the speakers in many of Dickinson's poems reveal a schism between personal spirituality and external displays of faith, such as "I prayed, at first, a little Girl, / Because they told me to –" (Fr546) and "Some – keep the Sabbath – going to Church / I – keep it – staying at Home –" (Fr236). In the latter poem, the speaker experiences and expresses her faith while in nature, where "'God' – preaches" directly to her in a "sermon [that] is never long." In this way, nature becomes a form of earthly heaven: "So – instead of getting to Heaven – at last – / I'm – going – all along!" Of course, Dickinson was not alone in equating God with Nature. Ralph Waldo Emerson, Nathaniel Hawthorne, Henry David Thoreau, and Walt Whitman expressed similar ideas, and Dickinson was also influenced by the writings and lectures of science professors at Amherst College as well as Reverend Charles Wadsworth, whom she once called "my closest earthly friend" (Ackmann 215). Yet Dickinson's speakers do not always find solace in nature as a stand-in for God's presence. In fact, feelings of frustration arise when God seems hidden: "Of Course – I prayed – / And did God Care?" (Fr581). She questions what she portrays as Christianity's blanket request for forgiveness: "For what, he is presumed to know – / The Crime, from us, is hidden –" (Fr1675). As Shira Wolosky points out, "For Dickinson . . . as for Melville and Hawthorne, Scripture seems to conceal rather more than it reveals. She questions that the world as word pronounces its Creator. She equally questions that God's written word does so" (139). Roger Lundin calls Dickinson's questioning the ability to "entertain contradictory religious ideas as possibilities, even as she resisted committing to them as definitive beliefs. . . . Late in life, Dickinson memorably described the to-and-fro process involved in this ceaseless consideration of possibilities: 'On subjects of which we know nothing, or should I say *Beings* – . . . we both believe, and disbelieve a hundred times an Hour, which keeps Believing nimble' (L750)" (151). Ultimately, as Neil Scheurich states, "Dickinson uncannily points to the . . . unknowability and ineffability of the spiritual" (191).

Scholars have struggled to determine Dickinson's religious beliefs and whether her poems reveal them because of "the countless beguiling and bewildering things Dickinson herself had to say about the God who may, or may not, exist" (Lundin 149–150). She "oscillates playfully, yet with a deadly seriousness, between affirmation and denial, and any attempt to pin down her beliefs may leave a reader feeling simultaneously beckoned by meaning and baffled by mystery" (150). Dickinson's varied speakers reflect an ambivalence that the poet herself most likely felt. As Scheurich explains, "One can say that for Dickinson spirituality is not easy belief in God, for she takes the physical world, and its lack of overwhelming evidence of further realities, quite seriously. However, neither is it the case that she can dismiss the possibility of faith altogether" (193). As Wolosky relates, "The world of Dickinson's poetry remains pressed between the invisible and visible, the unspoken and the spoken, in a tension she cannot resolve" (171).

Paula Bennett alludes to Dickinson's lack of faith in faith when she identifies "the poet's recognition that it is our ignorance and fear, not our eventual salvation, our sorrow and pain, not our future bliss, that in religious terms comprise the defining conditions of our lives" (80–81). However, Bennett says, "For Dickinson to abandon totally a belief in an afterlife (a belief in God's saving hand) would have been tantamount to giving up hope that we might have any 'home' at all" (81). I would argue, though, that in the poems in which God does appear, he does not appear as a savior but as an all-seeing, all-knowing deity. For example, Dickinson portrays this omniscient God in "Only God – detect the Sorrow –" (Fr692) and "My God – He sees thee –" (Fr1168). Equating Truth with God, "His Twin identity" (Fr795), Dickinson determines that they are equals and will share a "Co-Eternity –," thus proposing that God and Truth are forces in the universe, possibly even forces of nature, that can carry us to new levels of consciousness but cannot save us from ourselves. Claiming "Nature and God – I neither knew / Yet Both so well knew Me" (Fr803), Dickinson makes Nature and God equals as well. Perhaps, then, God, Truth, and Nature represent Dickinson's holy trinity; rather than questioning the existence of God, she redefined Him. As Jane Donahue Eberwein explains in "Emily Dickinson and the Calvinist Sacramental Tradition," the poet "recogniz[ed] occasions of grace in the natural world, within her own consciousness, and in her relationships with other people—demonstrating the multifarious ways in which spirit surcharges matter, thereby giving symbolic expression to her hope for immortality" and "convert[ing] doctrine into her own distinctively religious art" (104). Dickinson's skepticism stemmed less from a doubt in God than from an unwillingness to accept without question the Calvinist doctrine of her upbringing:

> Dickinson seems to have adopted a range of very different religions and antireligious positions. But that she could so vigorously toy with theology reinforces in itself arguments that she was deeply skeptical, as

much about Christianity as about any form of atheism. Although her thinking, as some scholars have shown, had been shaped by "a sentimental religious culture," she repudiated most of her society's platitudes and once remarked that "sermons on unbelief ever did attract me." (Gilbert 352)

Like Dickinson, 2Pac and the Notorious B.I.G. had their own versions of God. In 2Pac's "So Many Tears," he asks, "Is there heaven for G?" and "God can you feel me?" He entreats, "Take me away from all the pressure and all the pain / Show me some happiness again," seeing his life as time spent "in this cell" waiting for a "destiny" that he knows "is Hell." He asks God, "Where did I fail?" and grieves for "so many peers" that he has lost, "so many tears" that he has shed. In these prayer-like rap lyrics, 2Pac desires relief from a painful life marked by the fear that the afterlife may be worse. Likewise, in "The Heart asks Pleasure – first –" (Fr588), Dickinson's speaker asks for an "excuse from Pain – / And then – those little Anodynes / That deaden suffering." If painkillers do not work, perhaps "to go to sleep" is the only remedy. The final option, "if it should be / The will of it's Inquisitor" (i.e., God), is "The privilege to die." In contrast to the hell that 2Pac imagines, Dickinson's "The Heart asks Pleasure – first –" presents death as a peaceful relief from life's suffering, yet this "privilege" is a fate determined by God's "will" alone.

Gangsta rap, as Robert Tinajero explains, is "a subgenre of rap music . . . known mainly for its crude and violent rhetoric [but] also contains a vast amount of religious discourse and imagery" (315). Tinajero says that this "may be seen as an incompatible paradox to some, but rhetorical analysis reveals a complicated and layered connection in which the producers of gangsta rap, and those who strongly identify with its message, attempt to reconcile personal and social marginalization with aspects of religious thought" (315). The invocation of Jesus in many gangsta rap lyrics could also seem inconsistent with the rejection of organized religion that is characteristic of gangsta rappers. As Tinajero proposes,

> An interesting aspect of gangsta rap's religious rhetoric is that while it embraces the life of Jesus and aspects central to religious thought such as heaven, hell, justice, redemption, and meaning in suffering, there is a strong mistrust of organized and established religion. Gangsta rap's theology, therefore, is centred on the person of Christ, specifically on His suffering, but not religion centred. That is to say, while many gangsta rappers embrace the life and suffering of Jesus—and often display this attitude through visual and textual rhetoric—they do not embrace the entity of organized religion nor live what most would recognize as religious lives. (324)

The mistrust of organized religion present in gangsta rap aligns with Dickinson, who favored keeping the Sabbath at home. The Notorious B.I.G. shows his uncertainty about whether prayer will help him and his distrust of religion in "If I Should Die Before I Wake": "With my hands gripped, praise the Lord shit / Our father, if I should die before I wake." Just as child mortality was all too common in Dickinson's time, hence the teaching of "Now I Lay Me Down to Sleep" to nineteenth-century children, so is black youth mortality a reality in our time. As incongruent as nineteenth-century child mortality may seem with today's gangsta rap, it makes sense within the context of a very real fear of death before one's time and the attempt to comfort one's self before going to sleep and possibly not waking up. This preparation is similar to the precautions African American parents teach their African American children, particularly sons, for responding to police officers. The precautions are meant to protect but also to warn that death can result from a lack of compliance or simply having one's words or actions misunderstood. The ability to elude death becomes an accomplishment. In fact, Dickinson's words could serve as a gangster credo: "To be alive – is Power – / Existence – in itself –" (Fr876). Living to shoot another day is proof of a gangster's prowess and skill in the "thug" life. This keeps a "G" motivated to hustle and not have too much skin in the game; it is the shield that allows him to go into battle. Eithne Quinn identifies "two broad sets of archetypal protagonists" in gangsta rap: "the nihilistic gangbanger and the enterprising hustler" (92). One can live within the other.

The Notorious B.I.G. begins "You're Nobody (Til Somebody Kills You)" like a prayer with Psalm 23:4, as spoken by Puff Daddy, certain that he will have nothing to fear as God accompanies him on his journey into the afterlife. He anticipates his own death and "climb[ing] the ladder to success escalator style," ascending to heaven and the immortality that is assured with his words: "I spit phrases that'll thrill you / You're nobody 'til somebody kills you." As Dickinson describes, "Death" can "buy" you a "Room – / Escape from Circumstances – / And a Name –" (Fr644B). Thus, death provides space, escape, and a name that will live on. In the Notorious B.I.G.'s "Living in Pain," which also features 2Pac, Mary J. Blige, and Nas, Blige sings in the rap's chorus,

> Is anybody listening and tell me can you see this darkness surrounding me
> Now it's getting colder heavy on my shoulder and it's getting hard to breathe
> And it's gettin' blurry, I'm gettin' worried cause it's gettin' hard to see
> When you're living in the house of pain.

Unlike the bravado of "You're Nobody (Til Somebody Kills You)" and "Hypnotize," with the

> Condo paid for, no car payment
> At my arraignment, note for the plaintiff,
> 'Your daughter's tied up in a Brooklyn basement'
> Face it: not guilty—that's how I stay filthy,

"Living in Pain" acknowledges the fear and pain that come from feeling that your untimely death is inevitable. Even after the braggadocio of those four lines from "Hypnotize," the fifth line acknowledges the possibility of having to pay the consequences: "Richer than Richie, till you niggas come and get me." Perhaps a belief in Jesus, if not religion, is the only salvation for one who imagines his own death and who knows a sudden, violent death is inevitable yet unknowable. It is the suspense in waiting for death that is the real killer for the gangster, as Dickinson aptly explains: "Suspense – is Hostiler than Death – / Death – tho'soever Broad" because Death "cannot increase" and "Suspense – does not conclude –" (Fr775). In lines that could be from gangsta rap, Dickinson describes how suspense "perishes – to live anew / But just anew to die –." It is "Annihilation – plated fresh / With Immortality –." This suspense before death also appears in "Twas Crisis – All the length had passed –," where Dickinson refers to "That dull – benumbing time" when the "instant" is "holding in it's Claw / The privilege to live" or, alternatively, "Warrant to report the Soul / The other side the Grave" (Fr1093). With this life hanging in the balance, the "Muscles" and "Will" "grapple" while the "Spirit [shakes] the Adamant" but, alas, cannot "make it feel." Dickinson then describes how "The Second poised – debated – shot –" while "Another, had begun –," bringing to mind a pistol duel, which ends with "a Soul / Escap[ing] the House unseen –." No matter how hard one strives to stay alive, the poem implies, an instant can decide our fates. This vulnerability to death is the type that Scheurich sees in Dickinson's poetry: "For her, spirituality is not primarily about a deity, but rather about the peculiarly human situation in the universe. She captures spirituality in its most primordial manifestations, drawing upon the basic facts of having a vulnerable body in an inscrutable world" (193).

This fumbling in the dark toward an often unknowable, unreachable God is a recurrent theme in Dickinson's poetry. In "Father – I bring thee – not myself –" (Fr295B), she appears to criticize a God who will not hold "the departed Heart" that she "had not strength to hold –," asking, "Is it too large for you?" In "What is – 'Paradise' –" (Fr241), she wants an answer to the question of whether God exists, claiming, "You are sure there's such a person / As 'a Father' – in the sky –," and she seeks reassurance: "So if I get lost – there – ever – / Or do what the Nurse calls 'die' – / I shant walk the 'Jasper' – barefoot –." She wants to be certain that "Ransomed folks – wont laugh at me –," speculating, "Maybe – 'Eden' a'nt so lonesome / As New England used to be!" Dickinson's use of quotation marks around the words "a Father," "Jasper" (a heavenly building stone), and "Eden" could represent a radical questioning of concepts promised by Calvinist teachings. As Eberwein explains, even though the poet "called frequently, imaginatively, and memorably upon the idea of sacrament," she "virtually disregarded" certain "religious concepts emphasized within her culture . . . foremost among them the idea of total human depravity . . . [dispensing] with the concern for sin and fear of damnation that were emphasized within her church" ("Emily Dickinson and the Calvinist Sacramental Tradition," 89–90). In a much later poem, Dickinson's speaker argues that God is missing: "Those – dying . . . went to God's Right Hand –," a hand that is "amputated now" and a God that "cannot be found –" (Fr1581). This search for God is what Eberwein describes as Dickinson's "quest for assurance of immortality" (90), which is the "driving question" of her life and "the one great promise of Christianity that she kept testing in her poems, letters, and conversations" (104).

For 2Pac and the Notorious B.I.G., their very survival depends on the will of God. For example, 2Pac expresses gratitude to God after being "caught in the crossfire" but, in effect, dodged a bullet when he kept his life. As he states in "Letter 2 My Unborn," "I got shot five times, but I'm still breathin' / Living proof there's a God if you need a reason." The Notorious B.I.G. pointedly asks, "How many shots does it take, to make my heart stop / and my body start to shake, if I should die before I wake?" ("If I Should Die Before I Wake"), and 2Pac knows, "The power of a gun can kill" ("Power of a Smile"). Guns are necessary in gangsta rap as a reflection of their experiences, and surviving gunshots is often referred to as a mark of manliness. Guns can bring power and respect but only from one's peers. Guns—real or in rap lyrics—do not help black men in the dominant society, which has the power to incarcerate them for life for even minor crimes, using a prison system defined by slavery and designed to keep black men separate from white society (Stevenson). As 2Pac explains,

> I've been trapped since birth, cautious, 'cause I'm cursed
> And fantasies of my family, in a hearse
> And they say it's the white man I should fear
> But, it's my own kind doin' all the killin' here. ("Only God Can Judge Me")

In their references to the types and numbers of guns they have and how they use them, gangsta rappers are asserting power in a society that severely limits their options, and often these powerful, violent personas become reality. As Michael Eric Dyson points out, "Too often for gangsta rappers, life does indeed imitate and inform art" (175). Bell hooks explains how, in his memoir *The Ice Opinion*, Ice T describes this life of crime's appeal:

> "Crime is an equal-opportunity employer. It never discriminates. Anybody can enter the field. You don't need a college education. You

don't need a G.E.D. You don't have to be any special color. You don't need white people to like you. You're self-employed. As a result, criminals are very independent people. They don't like to take orders. That's why they get into this business. There are no applications to fill out, no special dress codes. . . . There's a degree of freedom in being a criminal." (28)

Although Ice T does not address the loss of freedom that occurs in prison, the dependence a criminal may have on his or her clients, associates, and family to keep the business running, or the lack of ability to move freely in one's own community due to fears of revenge or retribution, he makes it clear that crime is perhaps the only career that does not require kowtowing to a superior; crime appeals to young black men because of the freedom it brings.

Dickinson's gun references do not come anywhere close to their prolific use in gangsta rap. However, the gun is a central figure in one of Dickinson's most powerful and difficult poems, "My Life had stood – a Loaded Gun –" (Fr764). The speaker is a gun that has the "power to kill, / Without the power to die," which Joanne Dobson calls "an ironic fate: allowed power, but doomed to an unending eternity of destructiveness" (120), the type of fate that gangsta rappers refer to. The gun itself is a symbol of power, particularly a masculine power. According to bell hooks, "Gangsta culture is the essence of patriarchal masculinity. Popular culture tells young black males that only the predator will survive" (27). Gangsta rappers conflate themselves with guns, as in 2Pac's "Young black male! / (Hard like an erection)" ("Young Black Male") and the Notorious B.I.G.'s "Machine Gun Funk": "So you wanna be hardcore / With your hat to the back, talkin' bout the gats in your raps / But I can't feel that hardcore appeal." This hardness allows the gangster wannabe to believe that he will be bulletproof, but experienced gangsters know it is an illusion—guns only convey a temporary power and carry the risk of disempowerment at the hands of the dominant culture.

While rappers refer to the literal power of a gun to kill, Dickinson is referring to words rather than the gun itself; it is words that have the power to kill without the power to die. In her creation of poetry in general and this haunting poem about the power of language in particular, Dickinson was "capitalizing on a technique that women have always known and used, for survival, using the imagination as a space in which to create some life other than their external situation . . . [and] make art from it" (Juhasz 137). David T. Porter believes "the gun . . . is the emblem of her inordinate power of language" (quoted in Dobson 119). Indeed, the poet is the "gun" who "shoots" the words like bullets. This "gun-voice," as Dobson calls it, "embodies a superb ability and a pressing need to speak, filtered through a profound culturally conditioned anxiety about the acceptability of telling what she may well have considered deviant personal experience" (119). Gangsta rappers know their experiences deviate from the socially acceptable, and words are their way to not only broadcast it beyond their community but also as a means of becoming rich and famous: "trying to make a profit out of living in this sin" (2Pac, "Shorty Wanna Be a Thug"). As successful rappers, they can boast about their crimes, indict the police for their brutality, and ultimately portray law enforcement as impotent: "Got the police bustin' at me / But they can't do nothing to a G" (2Pac, "Ambitionz Az a Ridah"). Dickinson also knew the dangers of deviance, as Dobson explains: "For Dickinson, as for other women writers of her time, articulation of the self was a venture fraught with obscure dangers" (119). Yet writing also provided a sense of relief and control in a chaotic, violent world, particularly during the Civil War. As Ackmann explains, "It's hardly surprising that Dickinson wrote with such ferocity during the Civil War. High emotion fueled her. She turned to writing poetry in times of joy and love, and especially in hours of anguish. 'I must keep "gas" burning,' she wrote, 'to light the danger up' [L281]" (xxi).

Gangsta rappers also understand the power of words and use them as weapons in their raps, even in rivalries with one another. The lives of both 2Pac and the Notorious B.I.G. ended with drive-by shootings, a fate that both men likely recognized as a possibility. As Aimé Ellis states, "Black men (and women) have long been forced to make sense of their lives (and, in some cases, inescapable fates) from within a culture of terror committed to their annihilation" (94). In "Ready to Die," the Notorious B.I.G. says to life, "Bye bye, I was never meant to live / Can't be positive, when the ghetto's where you live." He claims that he was "never meant to be / Livin' like a thief, runnin' through the streets." From the day he was born, he claims, this has been his destiny. In seeing their peers killed, these rappers also have visions of their own mortality, as 2Pac asks in "Me Against The World": "The question is will I live?" A few lines later, he asks, "What's the use?" He knows he is "headed for danger, don't trust strangers." He wonders about the point of living when "No one in the world" loves him and "no one notices the youth" unless they are "shootin'." Perhaps alluding to a solitary game of Russian roulette or preparing to go up against an enemy, he remarks that he "Put[s] one in the chamber whenever I'm feeling this anger." 2Pac concludes, "It's just me against the world, baby."

Gangsta rappers also use words to flaunt the wealth and status that their rapping abilities have helped them achieve, and their lyrics reflect an awareness that an increase in status often correlates to an increase in being targeted. The Notorious B.I.G. says to his fellow "G"s, "Know you'd rather see me die than to see me fly" ("Mo Money Mo Problems"). Similarly, 2Pac knows he is

> caught up in the game, dress code changed
> Packin' 40 Glocks, contain 'em or rearrange
> All that jealousy and envy comin' from my enemies
> While I'm sippin' on Rémy. ("Picture Me Rollin'")

Gangsta rappers' references to the cash and luxury items they possess do not evoke pain and suffering, but this materialism serves as compensation for the loneliness and lack of love they describe, the kind of suffering that motivates one to create art. Scheurich explores the role of anguish in Dickinson's poetry, describing how her "work represents an exploration of the complex effects of suffering upon human action and aspiration. On the one hand, pain and despair have the potential to rob us of human capacities and reduce us to physical nature, but on the other they can be a stimulus to extraordinary creativity and insight; suffering leads alternatively to vigor or to prostration" (194). Whereas Dickinson found comfort in nature, 2Pac and the Notorious B.I.G. display a comfort that comes from conspicuous consumption and being the envy of other "G"s. Their art is their truest passion and source of satisfaction. In their world and Dickinson's, as different as they are, words represent the only way to achieve a form of immortality:

> A word is dead, when it is said
> Some say –
> I say it just begins to live
> That day (Fr278)

Creating art brought solace and the realization that their words would indeed live on, no matter what life had in store for them. As Dickinson writes, "The Poets light but Lamps – / Themselves – go out –" (Fr930).

In a poem portraying words as weapons, Dickinson refers to "a word" that "bears a sword" that "Can pierce an armed man –" (Fr42B). This word "hurls it's barbed syllables / And is mute again –." In this case, the pen is not mightier than the sword but used like one; in the second stanza, Dickinson takes the weapon metaphor one step further to compare the wordsmith to "the keenest marksman! / The most accomplished shot!" And who is on the receiving end of the bullet? The last two lines state that "Time's sublimest target / Is a soul 'forgot'!" This leaves the reader to wonder whether Dickinson was referring to the power of words collectively or a certain word, such as *mortality*. In another extended metaphor, Dickinson imagines a war of words in which "My friend attacks my friend!" in a "Battle picturesque!" before "I turn Soldier too, / And he turns Satirist!" (Fr103). "Had I a mighty gun," she claims, "I think I'd shoot the human race / And then to glory run!" In trying to outwit her opponent with his own weapon, satire, Dickinson shows the power of words to kill. This speculation about shooting the human race is obviously metaphorical in Dickinson's poetry, referring to killing with satire rather than gunfire, but in its threat of mass destruction, it is truly radical, even gangsta-like, which is an interesting way of thinking about Dickinson, a poet who "has been called everything from 'the outlaw of Amherst,' 'the best friend of reclusive English majors,' and 'an intellectual terrorist'" (Ackmann xxiii).

As a woman from a prominent family with a room of her own, Emily Dickinson had no reason to believe that she would be killed or feel the need to kill in defense. She even witnessed her brother Austin avoid that risk when a stand-in was paid to take his place in the Civil War. However, despite this sheltering, Dickinson was acutely aware of death through violence: "When the Ball enters, enters Silence – / Dying – annuls the power to kill –" (Fr616). As Sandra Gilbert relates, "The reclusive Myth of Amherst had, in her fashion, been deeply affected by the conflict whose carnage left so many dead" (364). Indeed, it is likely that this "national, political, and moral crisis . . . severely challenged her faith" more than any other single event in her life (Eberwein, "Dickinson's Local, Global, and Cosmic Perspectives," 38). As Cristanne Miller points out, "In some poems, Dickinson is profoundly critical of the self-righteousness of war rhetoric, with its martyrology and strident patriotism, and she does not participate in the widespread celebration of an exaggerated masculinity of valor and strength, express open patriotism, or write about the destiny of the nation. In others, however, she uses the popular war-time discourse of salvation and sentimental registers" (149). For example, "It feels a shame to be Alive – / When Men so brave – are dead –" (Fr524) "is written in unambiguous response to the war," and Dickinson "both evokes and disturbs the pieties of war martyrology while expressing the guilty gratitude of a civilian to soldiers" (Miller 150). Having envied "the Distinguished Dust – / Permitted – such a Head –," the speaker describes the "price" as "great – Sublimely paid –" and asks "Do we deserve – a Thing –" (such as "Liberty") "That lives – like Dollars – must be piled / Before we may obtain?" The speaker then questions whether "we that wait" are of "sufficient worth – / That such Enormous Pearl / As life – dissolved be – for Us – / In Battle's – horrid Bowl?" The concluding stanza states that "It may be – a Renown to live –," but there is a holiness in a soldier's ultimate sacrifice: "the Men who die –" are "Saviors" who "Present Divinity –" to the rest of us. As Miller explains, "While Dickinson never suggests that war itself is apocalyptic or sacred, several of her poems present soldiers as sanctified by their sacrifice" (150).

In "Soulja's Story," 2Pac portrays a different kind of soldier, one who struggles for respect and survival in what Walter Edwards calls a "battle against the system" (66). The rapper asks, "Is it my fault, just cause I'm a young black male?" In 2Pac's "Thugz Mansion," death does not occur nobly. "Tired of gettin' shot at" and "Tired of gettin' chased by the police and arrested," he admits, "I cry at times" and even "once contemplated suicide," but the only thing that stopped him was his "momma's eyes." He describes a struggle that "no one knows," only seeing "the trouble" and how hard it is to "carry on when no one loves you." "Praying hard for better days," he promises to "hold on." As Edwards explains,

> Tupac describes the oppressive life of a thug: the continuous dehumanizing harassment by police often leading to fatal confrontations; the constant pressure to assert his manhood by fighting or shooting individuals who disrespect him; the fugitive existence; the sense of hopelessness; the inevitable incarceration; and the frequent contemplation of suicide as the manly response to the humiliation of prison life. (65)

In "Born Again (Intro)," the Notorious B.I.G. speculates about his mortality: "Ten years from now, where do I want to be?" He answers, "I wanna be just livin' man / Just living comfortably." Then he considers what is most likely: "Ten years, I don't think I will see it . . . That shit ain't promised, man / I don't think my luck is that good, I hope it is / But if it ain't, so be it, I'm ready." Similarly, in "Everyday Struggle," the Notorious B.I.G. remarks that:

> I don't wanna live no more
> Sometimes I hear death knockin' at my front door
> I'm livin' every day like a hustle, another drug to juggle
> Another day, another struggle.

As Tinajero explains, "Themes of struggle and marginalization are not surprising, considering that a vast majority of this music, and consequently the gangsta rap ethos, are created mostly by poor racial minorities, especially African Americans and Latinos" (318). In "Trapped," 2Pac says, "Even a smooth criminal one day must be caught / Shot up or down with the bullets that he bought." Even if they are eventually able to leave prison, they will be released into a system that is designed to keep them in an endless cycle of violence, death, and incarceration, "coming out worse than they went in." Having survived is a badge of honor: "So many battlefield scars while driven in plush cars" (2Pac, "Ambitionz Az a Ridah"). Edwards attributes 2Pac's quick rise to fame with his first solo album, *2Pacalypse Now*, to the album's ability to "focus fiercely and unrelentingly on the experiences, characters, issues, social philosophy and drama of the Black neighborhoods Tupac had grown up in and knew intimately. Thus, his work achieved an immediacy and connectivity with his audience" (65). Charis Kubrin's study provides an overview of the social, political, and economic factors surrounding the rise of rap, which helps explain why both rappers and their audiences are drawn to descriptions of the thug life: "[E]conomic restructuring and punitive criminal justice initiatives have worsened conditions in the inner city in the last few decades. In their songs, rappers frequently make reference to the increasingly harsh conditions of what they call 'the ghetto'" (445). Consider, for example, the scene described by 2Pac in "Outlaw":

> 'Cause all I see is, murder murder, my mind state
> Preoccupied with homicide, tryin' to survive through this crime rate
> Dead bodies at block parties, those unlucky bastards
> Gunfire now they require may be closed casket.

The themes of urban violence, police brutality, and the plausibility of an early death communicate "anger, outrage and 'realness' to audiences of young, urban Blacks" (Edwards 65), causing some scholars to see rap as poetry "of the contemporary urban scene," "as a vehicle for telling the history of African American culture," "as an expressive artistic outlet for a marginalized urban social bloc," and as "an art form that reflects the nuances, pathology, and most importantly, the resilience of America's black ghettos" (Kubrin 433–434).

Without a doubt, death plays a central role in the "urban scene" of rap music; consequently, notions of the afterlife permeate gangsta rap lyrics, a subject that also captivated Dickinson. "Immortality," in fact, is what she called "the Flood subject" in an 1866 letter to T. W. Higginson (L319). In "Going to Heaven!" (Fr128B), Dickinson's speaker exclaims that she does not know when and pleads "do not ask me how!" She responds to an unidentified questioner, "Indeed I'm too astonished / To think of answering you!" The speaker seems to have just realized that she has secured a place in heaven, but she cannot provide any information beyond that fact. Her suggestion of "Perhaps you're going too!" recalls "I'm Nobody! Who are you?" (Fr260), not only in its rhyme scheme but also in its modest proposal, particularly in the lines that follow: "If you sh'd get there first / Save just a little place for me," assuring the conversation partner that "The smallest 'Robe' will fit me / And just a bit of 'Crown' –." In "Thugz Mansion," 2Pac imagines heaven as a more grandiose place where he can be with "chil'ren, dead homies and family" in a "sky high, iced out paradise, in the sky," a "chromed out mansion in paradise, in the sky." Truly a gangster's paradise, this is a nirvana where he and his "homies" are free from fear in a place where no police are allowed. 2Pac wants all that he was denied in real life for himself and his friends, and the potential that gangsta rappers see in the afterlife may contribute to the bravado and fearlessness of death that they often describe in their lyrics.

In a poem written around 1884, Dickinson's speaker beckons to death and imagines herself in the grave, entreating, "give me back to Death – / The Death I never feared" (Fr1653). The speaker is unafraid of death itself, but she does regret the loss of a connection with someone, of being "deprived of thee." In the opening line, the speaker implies death is a place where she has already been, similar to the death in life to which gangsta rappers refer. In fact, the speaker is able to "breathe" in her "own Grave" "And estimate it's size –." The fascinating final lines imply that death is a space that "is all that Hell can guess" and "all that Heaven was –." It is significant that death is not where Heaven *is* but *was*, which could mean "Heaven" was life on earth with the person the speaker feared being deprived of. In a much earlier poem that is one of Dickinson's most famous, the speaker personifies death as a gentlemanly carriage driver: "Because I could not stop for Death – / He kindly stopped for me – / The Carriage held but just Ourselves – / And Immortality" (Fr479). She describes a leisurely ride in which the speaker and death pass a school, a field of grain, the setting sun, and finally a house, or grave, that represents eternity. From the first line, Dickinson presents death as inevitable, implying that it is not up to us when we "go." Our carriages will arrive when it is our turn, and death will be cordial ("kindly") and patient: "We slowly drove – He knew no haste." The speaker realizes there is no point in resisting: "I had put away / My labor and my leisure too, / For His Civility –," paying death the respect he deserves. In this poem, Dickinson shows us not a journey *to* death but a journey *with* death to an unknown (and unknowable) destination. As Daneen Wardrop describes, "The figure of death allows [Dickinson] to plumb states of consciousness and explore concepts that might not otherwise be representable—among them despair, spiritual doubt, meaninglessness, timelessness, and cessation of knowing" (65). For gangsta rappers, death is a destination for which you can try to be prepared but which will arrive unannounced: "Takin' private planes, tryin' to survive the game / For all my homies that'll never be alive again / All he promised us is death" (2Pac, "Ballad of a Dead Soulja"). When the Notorious B.I.G. asks, "Can I live 'til my last day?" ("Last Day"), he refers to eluding death. "Gettin' money in the fast way" is to try to stay at least one step ahead of death, just as taking a private plane is a way to use money to insulate one's self from mortality. "Either you ridin' or you dyin'" in the gangster life, either "Gettin' money" or "runnin' from the Feds." The only way to stay alive is to outrun and outwit your enemies, which include other gangsters, law enforcement, and the government; there is no time for a leisurely ride in a carriage. Bell hooks explains that "Every day black males face a culture that tells them that they can never really achieve enough money or power to set them free from racist white tyranny in the work world. . . . Contrary to the notion that black males are lured by the streets, mass media in patriarchal culture has already prepared them to seek themselves in the streets, to find their manhood in the streets, by the time they are six years old" (26–27).

In another leisurely poem where death appears as a gentleman, Dickinson describes him as "the supple Suitor / That wins at last –" with "stealthy Wooing," an approach that is subtle at first but ends "with Bugles / And a bisected Coach / bear[ing] away in triumph" (Fr1470), evoking images of a royal wedding rather than a funeral. There is resistance implied in "wins at last," but the speaker is eventually seduced. The "pallid innuendoes / And dim approach" with which the seduction begins appear timid but are "brave at last" and end with a blaze of glory, or "triumph." In "I heard a Fly buzz – when I died –" (Fr591), an earlier and much more famous poem, Dickinson describes a deathbed scene as a rather mundane event. According to Wardrop, "Convention prompted nineteenth-century Calvinists to observe deathbed behavior because it might offer clues to the afterlife" (64). Although some of Dickinson's deathbed poems align with convention, many do not because they fail "to achieve a radiant, uplifting climax assuring the soul's salvation" (64). The focus in "I heard a Fly buzz," for example, is the fly, not the soul's ascent into heaven. Instead of "the King / Be[ing] witnessed – in the Room –... There interposed a Fly –... Between the light – and me –." Peter Boxall reads the first line of Dickinson's rebellious poem as making "the impossible claim, common to all posthumous narration, that one's own death has been achieved, that one has been able to experience and outlive one's own dying" (202). This exploration of one's own death is also commonplace in gangsta rap, although rappers generally describe rather violent deaths, most likely because that violence is found in their lives. As Jon Pareles states, "Many gangsta rappers prophesy their own deaths with bravado or fatalism. Sometimes that prophecy comes true" (A10). In gangsta rap, death comes in a blaze of guns; there is no subtlety, seduction, or stillness. In the "Long Kiss Goodnight," for example, it is simply "Time, time for you to die / As I kiss your ass goodnight" (the Notorious B.I.G.). Here, the gangster plays God in deciding another's time to die, the kill-or-be-killed ethos.

In "What if I say I shall not wait! / What if I burst the fleshly Gate – / And pass Escaped – to thee!" (Fr305), the speaker imagines her soul ascending to freedom, if not necessarily to heaven: "What if I file this mortal – off – / See where it hurt me – That's enough – / And step in Liberty!" Death is portrayed as a relief from pain, a theme that can be found throughout gangsta rap. Lines in the poem's third stanza ("Dungeons can call – and Guns implore – / Unmeaning – now – to me –") could be taken straight from a gangsta rap—there is a fearlessness in the face of death because it promises to take away the captivity and violence of life. More explicitly, in "Suicidal Thoughts," the Notorious B.I.G. reviews his sins and considers his death a penance for them, questioning whether his own mother would even miss him and imagining death not only as a relief from guilt but a relief to those who have known him and considered him "as the worst." After a lifetime of crime, from lying to his mother and stealing from her purse to drugs and extortion, he says, "I know my mother wished she got a[n] abortion," wondering if tears would come to her eyes if he died. "I swear to God," he says,

> I just want to slit my wrists and end this
> Throw the Magnum to my head, threaten to pull shit
> And squeeze, until the bed's completely red
> I'm glad I'm dead.

In "Life After Death (Intro)," the Notorious B.I.G. imagines coming back from death, hearing a voice, possibly God, saying, "I know you hear me . . . I know you hear me," telling him "You got too much livin' to do / Too much unfinished business," and "it ain't over." What this unfinished business includes is unclear. Revenge against a rival? A chance to start a new kind of life? Whatever the reason, this resurrection can be seen as a redemption, a rescue from death by God and perhaps a second life of crime: "I'm back reincarnated, incarcerated" (2Pac, "Ambitionz Az a Ridah"). Indeed, Dickinson proposes that "A Death blow is a Life blow, to Some, / Who till they died, did not alive become . . . but when / They died, Vitality begun" (Fr966B). There are fates worse than death; for some, vitality only begins when life ends.

Dickinson's work exhibits a longing to comprehend immortality, often describing death as a benevolent, patient figure. In contrast, gangsta rap lyrics imagine a sudden, violent death as an inevitability and hell as the most likely possibility, despite dreams of a thug paradise. Dickinson's work and gangsta rap lyrics, however, explore common themes, particularly the idea that poetry lives on, even after the poet has perished. Emily Dickinson wrote from a position of privacy and privilege, whereas 2Pac and the Notorious B.I.G., despite having achieved the wealth and fame that are often associated with security, knew their own vulnerability in a society that considers young black men the enemy. The disparities in their lives and work make the intersections all the more fruitful, revealing the power of language to unite and transcend.

Works Cited

The following abbreviations are used to refer to the writings of Emily Dickinson:

Fr *The Poems of Emily Dickinson*, edited by R. W. Franklin, Harvard UP, 1998. Citation by poem number.

L *The Letters of Emily Dickinson*, edited by Thomas H. Johnson and Theodora Ward, Harvard UP, 1958. Citation by letter number.

2Pac. "Ambitionz Az a Ridah." *All Eyez On Me*. Death Row Records, 1996.
----. "Ballad of a Dead Soulja." *Until the End of Time*. Amaru Entertainment, 2001.
----. "Letter 2 My Unborn." *Until the End of Time*. Amaru Entertainment, 2001.
----. "Me Against the World." *Me Against the World*. Interscope Records, 1995.
----. "Only God Can Judge Me." *All Eyez On Me*. Death Row Records, 1996.
----. "Outlaw." *Me Against the World*. Interscope Records, 1995.
----. "Picture Me Rollin'." *All Eyez On Me*. Death Row Records, 1996.
----. "Power of a Smile." *The Rose, Vol. 2*. Amaru Entertainment, 2005.
----. "Shorty Wanna Be a Thug." *All Eyez On Me*. Death Row Records, 1996.
----. "So Many Tears." *Me Against the World*. Interscope Records, 1995.
----. "Soulja's Story." *2Pacalypse Now*. Interscope Records, 1991.
----. "Thugz Mansion." *Better Dayz*. Interscope Records, 2002.
----. "Trapped." *2Pacalypse Now*. Interscope Records, 1991.
----. "Young Black Male." *2Pacalypse Now*. Interscope Records, 1991.
Ackmann, Martha. *These Fevered Days: Ten Pivotal Moments in the Making of Emily Dickinson*. W.W. Norton, 2020.
Bennett, Paula. *Emily Dickinson: Woman Poet*. U of Iowa P, 1991.
Boxall, Peter. "Blind Seeing: Deathwriting from Dickinson to the Contemporary." *New Formations: A Journal of Culture/Theory/Politics*, vol. 89-90, January 2017, pp. 192–211.
Dobson, Joanne. "Poem 754: The Unreadable Poem." *Emily Dickinson: A Celebration for Readers*, edited by Suzanne Juhasz and Cristanne Miller, Routledge, 2016, pp. 117–120.
Dyson, Michael Eric. "Gangsta Rap and American Culture." *The Hip Hop Reader*, edited by Tim Strode and Tim Wood, Pearson Education, 2008, pp. 172–181.
Eberwein, Jane Donahue. "Dickinson's Local, Global, and Cosmic Perspectives." *The Emily Dickinson Handbook*, edited by Gudrun Grabher, Roland Hagenbüchle, and Cristanne Miller, U of Massachusetts P, 1998, pp. 26–42.
----. "Emily Dickinson and the Calvinist Sacramental Tradition." *Emily Dickinson: A Collection of Critical Essays*, edited by Judith Farr, Prentice Hall, 1995, pp. 89–104.
Edwards, Walter. "From Poetry to Rap: The Lyrics of Tupac Shakur." *Western Journal of Black Studies*, vol. 26, no. 2, Summer 2002, pp. 61–70.
Ellis, Aimé J. *If We Must Die: From Bigger Thomas to Biggie Smalls*. Wayne State UP, 2011.
Gilbert, Sandra M. *Death's Door: Modern Dying and the Ways We Grieve*. W.W. Norton, 2006.
Hooks, bell. *We Real Cool: Black Men and Masculinity*. Routledge, 2004.

Juhasz, Suzanne. "The Landscape of the Spirit." *Emily Dickinson: A Collection of Critical Essays*, edited by Judith Farr, Prentice Hall, 1995, pp. 130–140.

Kubrin, Charis E. "'I See Death Around the Corner': Nihilism in Rap Music." *Sociological Perspectives*, vol. 48, no. 4, Winter 2005, pp. 433–459.

Lundin, Roger. "The Tender Pioneer in the Prairies of the Air: Dickinson and the Differences of God." *Religion & Literature*, vol. 46, no. 1, Spring 2014, pp. 149–157.

Miller, Cristanne. *Reading in Time: Emily Dickinson in the Nineteenth Century*. U of Massachusetts P, 2012.

Pareles, Jon. "Rapping, Living, and Dying a Gangsta Life." *New York Times*, 10 March 1997, p. A10.

Quinn, Eithne. *Nuthin' but a "G" Thang: The Culture and Commerce of Gangsta Rap*. Columbia UP, 2004.

Scheurich, Neil. "Suffering and Spirituality in the Poetry of Emily Dickinson." *Pastoral Psychology*, vol. 56, 2007, pp. 189–197.

Sewall, Richard B. *The Life of Emily Dickinson*. Harvard UP, 1974.

Stevenson, Bryan. "Why American Prisons Owe Their Cruelty to Slavery." *The New York Times Magazine*, 14 August 2019, www.nytimes.com/interactive/2019/08/14/magazine/prison-industrial-complex-slavery-racism.html.

The Notorious B.I.G. "Born Again (Intro)." *Born Again*. Bad Boy Records, 1999.

----. "Everyday Struggle." *Ready to Die*. Bad Boy Records, 1994.

----. "Hypnotize." *Life After Death*. Bad Boy Records, 1997.

----. "If I Should Die Before I Wake." *Born Again*. Bad Boy Records, 1999.

----. "Last Day." *Life After Death*. Bad Boy Records, 1997.

----. "Life After Death (Intro)." *Life After Death*. Bad Boy Records, 1997.

----. "Living in Pain (feat. 2Pac, Mary J. Blige, & Nas)." *Duets: The Final Chapter*. Bad Boy Records, 2005.

----. "Long Kiss Goodnight." *Life After Death*. Bad Boy Records, 1997.

----. "Machine Gun Funk." *Ready to Die*. Bad Boy Records, 1994.

----. "Mo Money Mo Problems." *Life After Death*. Bad Boy Records, 1997.

----. "Ready to Die." *Ready to Die*. Bad Boy Records, 1994.

----. "Suicidal Thoughts." *Ready to Die*. Bad Boy Records, 1994.

----. "You're Nobody (Til Somebody Kills You)." *Life After Death*. Bad Boy Records, 1997.

Tinajero, Robert. "Hip Hop and Religion: Gangsta Rap's Christian Rhetoric." *Journal of Religion and Popular Culture*, vol. 25, no. 3, Fall 2013, pp. 315–332.

Wardrop, Daneen. "Death, As Subject." *An Emily Dickinson Encyclopedia*, edited by Jane Donahue Eberwein, Greenwood, 1998, pp. 64–65.

Wolosky, Shira. *Emily Dickinson: A Voice of War*. Yale UP, 1984.

Chapter 4

"Some seek in Art –": Language and Literary Influence in Fascicle 30

Trisha Kannan
Independent Scholar

Abstract

Emily Dickinson's interest in the life and work of John Keats is no secret. In an 1862 letter to Thomas Wentworth Higginson, for example, she wrote, "You inquire my Books – For Poets – I have Keats – and Mr and Mrs Browning" (L261). Although "I died for Beauty –" (Fr448) is an overt reference to Keats's "Ode on a Grecian Urn," Dickinson most often alludes to literary precursors in subtle, complex ways. Thus, the Keatsian "echoes," as Elizabeth Petrino describes them, in Dickinson's work are easily overlooked, yet attending to them in the context of Fascicle 30 reveals the specific, positive influence that Keats had on Dickinson. In particular, the fascicle's poems address artistic immortality, poetic inspiration, the solace found in nature, and the undeniable, often bitter power of experience in ways that support Dickinson's sustained interest in Keatsian ideas, imagery, and language.

Key words: John Keats, transatlantic literature, fascicles, manuscript study

***

The fascicles of Emily Dickinson represent a complex, rich, and illuminating means of understanding the importance of context and intertextuality. The poems contained within the sheets of Fascicle 30 reveal a positive, specific relationship to John Keats in ways that have not been previously analyzed. The poems in their fascicle context disclose a direct correlation to Keats's "Nature and the Poets," "Fancy," "Fairy Song," "Bards of Passion and of Mirth," "Ode to a Nightingale," and "To Autumn." These connections highlight sources of poetic inspiration that Dickinson shared with Keats, such as nature, dreams, and human experience, both positive and negative. In addition, the Fascicle 30 poems explore notions of artistic immortality in ways that align with and reject the ideas in "I died for Beauty –" (Fr448), Dickinson's most overt reference to

Keats. Attending to Dickinson's Fascicle 30 poems elucidates the work of both poets and emphasizes the power of language to transverse time and space.

What Are the Fascicles?

In his Introduction to the 1998 variorum of *The Poems of Emily Dickinson*, R. W. Franklin[1] gives extensive details regarding "the most prominent part of the manuscripts that Lavinia Dickinson found in May 1886," which are the

> fascicles, her sister's own form of bookmaking: selected poems copied in ink onto sheets of letter paper that she bound with string. . . . In all Lavinia discovered forty bound fascicles, containing over eight hundred poems, and a good many fascicle sheets that had never been bound. These unbound groups, called *sets* following the terminology of *The Manuscript Books of Emily Dickinson* (1981), brought the total to over eleven hundred. (7)

The individual sheets of letter paper, called "fascicle sheets," were stacked one on top of another, rather than nestled. The earlier fascicles normally have four sheets, producing a booklet with eight leaves with text on both sides, and the later fascicles have a norm of six (Franklin, *Manuscript Books*, xi). "Sometimes the last poem ran over onto a separate leaf (twice onto the next full sheet) and on a few occasions onto a separate slip that was pinned, or in one case bound, into place. . . . To bind, Dickinson stacked the assembled sheets, with the overflow leaves (if any) in place, punched two holes through the group, threading it with string, tied on the front" (Franklin, 1998, 7). Dickinson began constructing the fascicles in 1858, and "the beginning of 1866 marked the effective end of fascicle making" (26). Franklin, who sees the fascicles as a means of keeping order or as a repository of poems from which she would make copies and send in letters, describes the non-fascicle manuscripts as "a proliferating disarray of scraps of paper":

---

[1] Franklin is the second editor to create a scholarly edition of Dickinson's complete poems. Thomas H. Johnson produced the first scholarly edition in 1955, and Franklin's revises Johnson's edition. Both Johnson and Franklin present the poems in an assumed chronological order based on paper, handwriting, poems included with dated letters, and other contextual evidence. Dickinson did not date any of her poems or fascicles. Franklin renumbered the poems 1–1789 in 1998, writing in the 1998 Introduction that "The present dating has had an advantage not enjoyed by *Poems* (1955) in that it was accomplished after the reconstruction of the fascicles . . . the fascicles and sets, containing about two thirds of the poems, have been a sturdier base upon which to study handwriting and assign dates than a series of individual manuscripts . . . The dating is of documents, not necessarily of the composition of poems" (38–39).

The next four years are without fascicles or sets or even many poems, only ten or twelve in each of the years from 1866 through 1869, almost like the silent years from 1855–1857. In 1870 she returned to making individual fascicle sheets (Sets 8–12, 15, 13–14), but it was an occasional occupation and lasted only until 1875. During these later years, except for the last two, when illness was debilitating, her output rose again, but it never reached earlier levels. She continued to work with first and second drafts and to produce retained copies prepared more formally, as if for a recipient. (26)

The fascicle poems are copied in ink, whereas later poems, or poems not on fascicle sheets, are often (but not always) in pencil. Dickinson's normal formula was to destroy earlier drafts, so while Franklin calls certain years "silent," he refers to a lack of manuscripts from that period; Dickinson could have been writing, of course, but we no longer have evidence of it.

In the nineteenth century, the fascicles were taken apart, and Dickinson's first editors—Mabel Loomis Todd and T. W. Higginson—selected poems to include in the volumes printed in 1890, 1891, and 1896. These first printed volumes divided Dickinson's poems into subject categories, such as Nature and Love; they were edited to conform to standards of punctuation and capitalization; and titles were added. In 1981, R. W. Franklin published *The Manuscript Books of Emily Dickinson*, which reestablished (as much as possible) the fascicle order and allowed readers to read the manuscripts themselves, rather than print transcriptions.[2] This ushered in a new era of Dickinson scholarship that focused on figuring out Dickinson's intentions with regard to her fascicle project. The earliest study of the fascicles to be published after the *Manuscript Books* is by William Shurr, who reads the 40 fascicles as indicative of a marriage between Dickinson and Henry Wadsworth. Although Shurr's study has been discredited because of the unfounded and unhelpful biographical focus, later critics also attempted to align the fascicles with Dickinson's life story. In *The Passion of Emily Dickinson*, for example, Judith Farr reads within Dickinson's work "cycles" of poems that describe her passion first for Susan Gilbert Dickinson and then for "Master," whom Farr believes is Samuel Bowles. Although Farr mentions the fascicles quite often and searches within them for these two narrative strands, her project is not a sustained focus on the fascicles. She writes,

---

[2] All of Dickinson's manuscripts are now available online through Harvard's *Emily Dickinson Archive*.

> the forty fascicles, together with a few unbound poems, talk about the beloved woman [Sue] in a fashion inconvenient to facile deductions about the chronology of events. For example, long after the beloved has been claimed by another [Austin], Dickinson's speaker rehearses heightened moments of their love as if these had just occurred. . . . Chronologically, then, Dickinson's story is random. Nevertheless, taken in their entirety, the poems for the beloved woman constitute a distinct narrative. (132)

Farr's observation that the fascicles are "chronologically random" aligns with Franklin's and prior editors' frustration at the lack of clear intent with regard to the fascicles. I am unconvinced by Farr's "story," although her use of the poems, in and out of their fascicle contexts, as a means to explore Dickinson's "desire for a life in art" aligns with the majority of twentieth-century criticism, which is to use Dickinson's poetry to fill in her biography and vice versa (Farr 30).

Similarly to Farr, Dorothy Huff Oberhaus attempts to find a narrative structure within a single fascicle, which she then applies to all the fascicles as well as to Dickinson's life. In the only book-length study on a single fascicle, Oberhaus reads Fascicle 40 as a three-part conversion narrative. Oberhaus applies the poetic content of this final fascicle back to the first fascicle to argue the fascicle project as whole tracks the protagonist's poetic and spiritual pilgrimage, culminating in the conversion narrative of the final fascicle. Oberhaus's reading of Fascicle 40 is to show the protagonist's attainment of true contentment in a spiritual as well as poetic union with Jesus Christ. Oberhaus examines the progress of the poet and the woman, arguing that the narrative of the fortieth fascicle shows how the protagonist, as the author of the fascicles, views her poetry to be not only inspired by but written for Christ. Oberhaus's study illuminates the textual influence of the Bible in Fascicle 40, yet her attempt to find a single "story" within the 40 fascicles remains unconvincing.

Within the past few decades, more fascicle scholarship has appeared, and these studies reflect the complexity of Dickinson's forty "books." In *Reading the Fascicles of Emily Dickinson: Dwelling in Possibilities,* Eleanor Heginbotham argues that "the fact of the fascicles deserves attention. Regardless of whether they were complete or finished or intended as prepublication studies, as self-publishing artifacts, as gifts, as scrapbooks, or as workbooks, they *exist*" (ix). Heginbotham studies individual fascicles to discover "what proximate poems can tell us about each other and what the selections—for they are that, it seems to me, rather than repositories—suggest about the concerns of their author at the moment she bound them together" (xi). Heginbotham explores Fascicle 21 in particular, focusing on "They shut me up in Prose –" and "This was a Poet –" to reveal the importance of the fascicle context. Heginbotham argues these two poems speak to each other across the page, each opening up interpretive possibilities for the other. . . . Here are two poems, both of them familiar to Dickinson readers as disparate entities; when explored together, however, . . . they become new artifacts by virtue of their proximity. (5)

Heginbotham argues that Fascicle 21 is where "Dickinson declared her aesthetic principles," which emphasize "the subversive and affective possibilities of poetry" (5,18). Heginbotham reads the central poems as declaring Dickinson's "aesthetic stance," which is "far from those of her contemporary 'fireside poets,' whose strictly metered, true-rhyming, nationalistic, and inspirational verse was rarely de-stilling or unsettling," while the "entire fascicle reflects the 'business' of the working poet" (18, 24). In discussing Dickinson's aesthetic principles and the business of poetry, Heginbotham notes the influence of Keats and Barrett Browning (among others), and several poems in Fascicle 21 can be read as references to these specific poetic precursors. "I died for Beauty –" (Fr448), for example, appears in Fascicle 21 and is Dickinson's most overt reference to the work of John Keats. The poem explores the relationship and significance of Beauty and Truth, and scholars have long established the poem's connection to Keats's "Ode on a Grecian Urn," particularly the urn's famous words that "'Beauty is truth, truth beauty.'"

Rather than highlighting poetic connections to several authors, as Heginbotham does to reveal Dickinson's "aesthetic principles" in Fascicle 21, Ann Swyderski traces the influence of a single author in the "Barrett Browning Fascicles," which are fascicles 26, 29, and 31. According to Franklin's 1998 variorum, Dickinson recorded the first elegy to Barrett Browning into Fascicle 26 around the summer of 1863, and the second and third into Fascicle 29 and Fascicle 31 about the second half of 1863. Dickinson's interest centers not only on Barrett Browning's work but on her status as a well-known woman poet. Swyderski shows that the "Barrett Browning Fascicles" "record [Dickinson's] evolving relationship with Barrett Browning. . . . Dickinson chose to embed these poems [the elegies] in gatherings of other poems which explore her own development as a woman and poet" (76–78).

In addition to Swyderski's work with the Barrett Browning fascicles and Heginbotham's with Fascicle 21, James Wohlpart discusses how Fascicle 22 exemplifies Dickinson's confrontation with nineteenth-century dichotomies, concluding that "the liberation" at the heart of the fascicle "subverts orthodox, religious views on redemption and can most clearly be defined as the establishment of interrelationships with the natural world and with other humans that enable her to transform the quotidian into the sacred" (55). In

"Emily Dickinson and the Gothic in Fascicle 16," Daneen Wardrop explores how the poems of Fascicle 16 reveal Dickinson's understanding and use of the Gothic. Wardrop argues that in "Fascicle 16 we can see particularly well how Dickinson works within an established genre, Gothicism, which by this time she is accustomed to using, in order to turn to more difficult questions of how an identity is formed" (142). William Doreski focuses on figurations of loss in Fascicle 27, and M. L. Rosenthal and Sally Gall focus on Fascicle 15 and Fascicle 16 to argue for a sequential movement, which compares to the modern poetic sequence. Robert Bray also finds a lyric sequence in Fascicle 18. In contrast to the fascicles containing narratives or sequences, Sharon Cameron argues Dickinson's manuscripts reveal postmodern concerns about what constitutes the identity of a poem. Cameron argues the variants[3] are not alternative possibilities but integral to the poem, and they represent Dickinson "choosing not to choose" one word or phrase over another. Cameron's argument as to Dickinson's lack of choice regarding a "final version" of the fascicle poems is based on considering the variants "as inclusive rather than substitutive" (63). Cameron views Dickinson as offering the variants in order to extend the identity of a poem and the possibilities of poetry. In Cameron's point of view, the variants, as well as their visual presence in the manuscripts, are imperative in any speculation regarding the identity of a Dickinson poem. Cameron explores in detail Fascicle 20 and Fascicle 16, but she views the fascicles overall as Dickinson's interest in what constitutes poetry: "[U]nity is not produced by reading Dickinson's lyrics in the fascicle context. . . . What is more radically revealed is a question about what constitutes the identity of the poem. . . . Dickinson's fascicles can rather be seen to embody the problem of identity" (4). A 2014 collection edited by Heginbotham and Paul Crumbley, appropriately titled *Dickinson's Fascicles: A Spectrum of Possibilities*, reveals the varied ways

---

[3] "Variants" is the term used to refer to the alternative words or lines in Dickinson's manuscripts. Dickinson wrote a small cross above a word or line to indicate variant possibilities, which would typically be added at the end of the poem. Cameron's theory about the operation of the variants contrasts with Franklin's belief that the variants indicate Dickinson's desire to keep the manuscripts private. According to Franklin's 1998 Introduction, "Dickinson's care in preparing the earliest fascicles, which admitted only completed poems, all their alternative readings resolved, shows the goal to have been a finished product. She used clean erasure, not overwriting or crossing out, and deftly squeezed in omitted letters. Before 1860, she did not revise them. The first appearances of extraneous writing are in Fascicle 5, where an omitted reading was transcribed in ink as an alternative (Fr121), and in Fascicle 7, where for two poems (Fr145, Fr159) an alternative was added in pencil. . . . As of Fascicle 9, in early 1861, they would have been unsuitable for circulation. The transcription, though in ink, was less careful, and the texts, now with unresolved readings, were not intended for others" (20).

more recent scholars have approached the fascicles. The book opens with a section from Cameron's 1992 *Choosing Not Choosing* because hers "was the first study of the fascicles that challenged readers to examine carefully the nonnarrative, indeterminate, and highly disruptive attributes of fascicle poems" (2). In contrast to earlier studies, most fascicle scholars now reject the idea that the fascicles are narratives, sequences, or even books, largely due to the fact that Franklin's reorganization of the manuscripts cannot be verified as exact. Franklin reconstructed the individual fascicles and ordered them according to the date around which the poems were copied into the fascicle. While the dating of stationery and the progression of Dickinson's handwriting provide clues as to the year a fascicle was created, the numbers 1–40 are otherwise arbitrary, meaning that "it is only arbitrarily that Fascicle 13 precedes Fascicle 14" (Cameron 16 n11). Mabel Loomis Todd, however, did keep track of the fascicles, and much of Franklin's reconstruction is based on her system.[4]

Alexandra Socarides, for example, believes the fascicles are not booklets of poetry and instead focuses on the fascicle sheet:

> Attending to how Dickinson made the fascicles reveals that she was working with a particular unit of construction—the fascicle sheet—and, in doing so, was already thinking about the very problems of narrative, sequence, fragmentation, and genre that Dickinson scholars have been struggling with for over a hundred years. Once we see that the fascicles aren't what we've always assumed them to be—books of lyric poems whose contents can be both extracted individually and read sequentially—then we will be able to identify what they are and what kinds of poems Dickinson copied in them. ("Dickinson, Higginson, and the Problem with Print" 2)

Rather than focusing on "the fascicles as something read," Socarides views "the fascicles as something made" ("Rethinking the Fascicles" 71), arguing that Dickinson uses the fascicle sheet to "formally address her own resistance to both the static lyric moment and an all-encompassing narrative" (89). Socarides concludes that the complexity and difficulty of the fascicles cause one "to rethink the boundaries between individual texts":

---

[4] Ruth Miller studied the fascicles before they were reestablished in 1981, and she details how Franklin's efforts came to be; see pages 247–332 of Miller's *The Poetry of Emily Dickinson*. Although Miller's claim about the fascicles following a "blueprint" has been proved untrue upon further study, she was the first to show a scholarly interest in the fascicles as artistic productions.

In the end, the fascicles may continue to avoid classification at every turn. Yet it is this very avoidance that opens up new questions that allow for a reexamination of the materials themselves, the assumptions that have been made about them, and the discourses that are the most useful when discussing both. (89)[5]

Dickinson's body of work, since there are *so many* possibilities inherent in only a handful of case studies or within a single fascicle, problematizes the assumptions that constitute literary identity, such as the need for clearly demarcated boundaries between genres. Socarides argues that the fascicle sheets reveal Dickinson's play with the limitations of print; she closely reads the poems in their manuscript fascicle page "to see some of the amazing relations Dickinson put into play," relations that print will always obscure ("Problem with Print" 6).[6]

Fascicle 30 and Literary Influence

Influenced by the work of fascicle and manuscript scholars, I read the six sheets of Fascicle 30 as revealing the sources of poetic inspiration shared by Dickinson

---

[5] Socarides expands upon her ideas in these earlier articles in her 2012 book *Dickinson Unbound: Paper, Process, and Poetics*, which is influenced by and converses with Virginia Jackson's pivotal 2005 work in *Dickinson's Misery: A Theory of Lyric Reading*. In her Introduction, Socarides writes, "In short, once we accept that Dickinson's poems have been misread lyrically, then the question that follows is what those poems were before that misreading" (5).

[6] Until 2016, when Cristanne Miller published *Emily Dickinson's Poems: As She Preserved Them*, the only way to read Dickinson's poems in their fascicle contexts was to read the poems in manuscript, either in Franklin's *Manuscript Books*, by accessing library holdings, particularly at Harvard, or eventually by looking at digital images in online collections. In many ways, Miller's approach to the fascicles is similar to Franklin's: the fascicles represent Dickinson's method of organization and preservation, rather than, as many manuscript scholars contend, selections with an artistic purpose. Miller's edition transcribes into print all the poems contained within the forty fascicles and the unbound sheets, as well as the "loose poems," and she follows the ordering of sheets that Franklin presented in *Manuscript Books*, with the revised dating information from the 1998 edition. The purpose of Miller's edition, as stated in the Preface, is "to present in easily readable form Dickinson's own ordering of the poems she bound into forty handmade booklets between 1858 and 1864, and of the poems she copied into unbound sheets between 1864 and 1875" (vii). Miller's edition is the first scholarly edition to print all of Dickinson's poems with attention to their organization in the fascicles and sets. "It is also the first annotated reading edition of her poems. And it is the first edition to include the alternative words and phrases Dickinson wrote on the pages of many of the poems she retained. It presents the poet at work" (vii).

and Keats: nature, reading and writing poetry, sleep and dreams, and the joy and pain of life on earth. It is well known that Dickinson read Keats, but the exact nature of Keats's influence on Dickinson has been the subject of scholarly debate for decades.[7] The most apt description was coined by Elizabeth Petrino in 2010—*echo*. Petrino writes, "Dickinson employed allusion and echo—to the images, sounds, and even cadences of other literary works—to write in an innovative, generative way" (80–81). On April 25, 1862, Emily Dickinson wrote to T. W. Higginson, "You inquire my Books – For Poets – I have Keats – and Mr and Mrs Browning" (L261). Higginson's "Letter to a Young Contributor," which appeared in the April 1862 edition of the *Atlantic Monthly*, inspired Dickinson's initial letter to him, which she sent on April 15, 1862, with the opening line, "Are you too deeply occupied to say if my Verse is alive?" (L260). Dickinson perhaps lists Keats first in her second letter because Higginson's essay discloses his high regard for Keats: "Keats himself has left behind him winged wonders of expression which are not surpassed by Shakspeare [*sic*], or by any one else who ever dared touch the English tongue" (403). After Dickinson's second letter to Higginson, no mention of Keats appears in the letters until September 1885, when Dickinson asks Forrest Emerson for any information regarding the "circumstances" of Helen Hunt Jackson's death and exclaims, "Oh had that Keats a Severn!" (L1018). Dickinson seems to recall Joseph Severn's essay "On the Vicissitudes of Keats's Fame," which appeared in the April 1863 edition of the *Atlantic Monthly*. Dickinson wishes to know the details of Jackson's "life's close" as thoroughly as Severn could recount Keats's final hours.

The last mention of Keats exists in a letter to the Norcross cousins written about March 1886. Johnson notes that the letter references *Endymion*, although the lines quoted are not exact to Keats's text: "Was your winter a tender shelter – perhaps like Keats's bird, 'and hops and hops in little journeys'?" (L1034). In

---

[7] Karl Keller, for example, posits that there is a Keatsian presence "somewhere" in Dickinson's poetry, and Joanne Diehl imagines Keats as an anxiety-producing father figure to Dickinson, although Diehl recognizes the positive outcome of this tension and reads Dickinson "within the context of the Romantic tradition" to reveal "the experimental daring and revolutionary character of Dickinson's achievement" (*Dickinson and the Romantic Imagination* 4). While multiple studies have also contextualized Dickinson within Anglo-American Romanticism, specific correlations to Keats have often been overlooked. For an entry point into Dickinson's relation to the Romantic/Transcendental tradition, see: Diehl's *Women Poets and the American Sublime*; Evan Carton's *The Rhetoric of American Romance*; Shira Wolosky's "Dickinson's Emerson: A Critique of American Identity;" Glauco Cambon's "Emily Dickinson and the Crisis of Self-Reliance;" Laura Gribbin's "Emily Dickinson's Circumference: Figuring a Blind Spot in the Romantic Tradition;" and Richard Brantley's *Experience and Faith: The Late-Romantic Imagination of Emily Dickinson*.

the *Atlantic Monthly* (September 1862), Higginson's essay "The Life of Birds" quotes Keats's *Endymion*: "If an innocent bird / Before my heedless footsteps *stirred and stirred / In little journeys*" (374; italics in original). Higginson's lines also vary slightly—italics added, a comma removed, "stirred" instead of "stirr'd"—from Keats's 1818 publication of *Endymion*, Book I, lines 698–700. The lines in Dickinson's letter could be from Higginson's essay, and thus the letter does not prove Dickinson's familiarity with *Endymion*, although Dickinson is alluding to the lines more than 20 years after the publication of Higginson's essay. Petrino notes that "Dickinson appears to have absorbed Higginson's reinterpretation of Keats's lines, so that it functions for her as an expression of tender shelter. She then further appropriates the original text and makes it her own; revising the original 'stirr'd' as 'hops' creates a more active, restless feel" (84).

The Dickinson family owned Charles A. Dana's *Household Book of Verse* (1860) and Robert Chambers's *Cyclopaedia of English Literature* (1844 and 1847).[8] Dana's collection is grouped by category, such as Poems of Nature, Poems of Childhood, and Poems of Love, and contains 14 poems by Keats, including "Nature and the Poets," "Fancy," "Fairy Song," "Bards of Passion and of Mirth," "Ode to a Nightingale," and "To Autumn," all of which have echoes in Fascicle 30. Chambers's *Cyclopaedia* includes nine poems by Keats, several of which also appear in Dana's collection, and an introduction to Keats's life and works, which quotes and contextualizes Lord Byron's description of Keats in *Don Juan*: "John Keats, who was killed off by one critique, / Just as he really promised something great, / If not intelligible, without Greek / Contrived to talk about the gods of late, / Much as they might have been supposed to speak" (quoted in Chambers 404).[9] Chambers's introduction to Keats explains:

> In 1818 Keats published his *Endymion, a Poetic Romance,* defective in many parts, but evincing rich though undisciplined powers of imagination. The poem was criticized, in a strain of contemptuous severity, by the Quarterly Review; and such was the sensitiveness of the

---

[8] See the Dickinson family library collection at Harvard's Houghton Library: EDR 442, EDR 443, and EDR 445. Samuel Bowles gave Dana's collection to Austin and Sue, Chambers's 1844 *Cyclopaedia* is inscribed "Sue H. Gilbert 1856," and the 1847 edition of the *Cyclopaedia* belonged to Emily's father. Although these books did not belong explicitly to Dickinson, her close relationship with Sue implies that she very likely accessed Keats's work through these texts.

[9] Dickinson could have read the lines in *Don Juan* as well. The Dickinson family owned *Letters and Journals of Lord Byron*, the four-volume collection of *The Works of George Gordon Byron* (1821), and an 1854 edition of Byron's collected works (EDR 112, EDR 492, and EDR 441, respectively).

young poet—panting for distinction, and flattered by a few private friends—that the critique embittered his existence, and induced a fatal disease. (402)

As Petrino notes, "Keats's life history as well as his poetic themes undoubtedly sparked her [Dickinson's] interest. . . . He idealized the craft of poetry and desired to be remembered as a poet, even though savage critical attacks and his impending death from tuberculosis made the likelihood of a long-lasting fame seem remote" (84–85). Petrino explains that "Dickinson's echoes of Keats . . . have often gone unnoticed, perhaps because they are not easily detectable unless the precursor and later texts are closely compared" (81). In addition, many of Dickinson's allusions or echoes are filtered through the influence of other writers. For example, of Keats's "I died for Beauty – but was scarce" (Fr448), Petrino argues that "Dickinson's familiarity with Keats's famous line came not only through her exposure to his poem, but also two other probable sources: Ralph Waldo Emerson's *Nature* (1836) and Elizabeth Barrett Browning's 'A Vision of Poets' (1844)" (85). Noting the influences of these other writers, both of whom were very important to Dickinson, Petrino concludes that "I died for Beauty–" explores the power of poetry in a way that incorporates the ideas of Keats, Emerson, and Barrett Browning: "Rather than asserting artistic immortality, as Keats does, Dickinson's poem highlights the finality of the grave for the philosopher and poet" (87). Petrino explains that the poem's ending line, where Dickinson's figures are "silenced by a lowly and creeping but living 'Moss,'" implies that "[u]nlike Barrett Browning, who argues that the poet achieves greatness in suffering and death, and Emerson, who contends that both artist and philosopher search for absolute knowledge, Dickinson shares with Keats a belief that the work, not the poet, is immortal" (88).

The sheets of Fascicle 30 address themes related to "artistic immortality" in ways that both support and reject the speaker's point of view in "I died for Beauty –." Fascicle 30 has six sheets, three of which contain three poems and three that have four:

Sheet One
No Crowd that has occurred (Fr653)
Beauty – be not caused – It is – (Fr654)
He parts Himself – like Leaves – (Fr655)

Sheet Two
I started Early – Took my Dog – (Fr656)
"Morning" – means "Milking" – to the Farmer – (Fr191B)
Endow the Living – with the Tears – (Fr657B)

Sheet Three
'Tis true – They shut me in the Cold – (Fr658)
The Province of the Saved (Fr659)
I took my Power in my Hand – (Fr660)
Some such Butterfly be seen (Fr661)

Sheet Four
I had no Cause to be awake – (Fr662)
I fear a Man of frugal Speech – (Fr663)
Rehearsal to Ourselves (Fr664)
The Martyr Poets – did not tell – (Fr665)

Sheet Five
I cross till I am weary (Fr666)
Answer July – (Fr667)
There is a Shame of Nobleness – (Fr668)

Sheet Six
An ignorance a Sunset (Fr669)
One Crucifixion is recorded – only – (Fr670)
The Sweetest Heresy received (Fr671)
Take Your Heaven further on – (Fr672)[10]

The sheets within Fascicle 30 reveal a contemplation of the power of poetry as well as the undeniable, bitter, and often dismal power of experience. The groupings of the poems reflect Dickinson's interest during these pivotal years— 1861 to 1863—in her work and life as a poet. She had been binding the fascicles since about 1858, had sought Higginson's opinion of her work in April 1862 and asked him to be her "Preceptor" in June 1862, had written three elegies to one of her favorite poets who died on June 30, 1861, and had read articles by Higginson (April and September 1862) and Severn (April 1863) that celebrated Keats's "winged wonders of expression." Severn's article may have been particularly inspirational because it explores issues of poetic immortality and fame, a topic of interest to Dickinson during these years, especially with regard to Barrett Browning. Severn states that American readers appreciated Keats

---

[10] The same stationery is used for fascicles 29, 30, and 31, and Franklin records in the 1998 variorum that these three fascicles were all created about the second half of 1863. In fact, the poems of Fascicle 30 follow Franklin's numbering from 653–672, with the addition of Fr191B, which appears on the second sheet, whereas the poems of Fascicle 31 are numbered 630–652; poems 673–679 are in Set 1, 680–699 are in Fascicle 32, and 610–629 are in Fascicle 29.

because they did not have the literary biases of England: "in America he has always had a solid fame, independent of the old English prejudices" (401). The article is not just about Keats but the power of Keats's memory and the continual influence that artists serve for other artists, a theme Dickinson explores in a few poems in the Fascicle 30 sheets. Severn declares, "as I write, I look back through forty years of worldly exchanges to behold Keats's dear image again in memory" (401). The mention of "forty years" reminds readers just how long ago Keats died, reinforcing the long-standing power and influence of Keats on Severn. The editorial note to the article emphasizes Severn's own literary fame (he "scarcely needs introduction") as well as the symbiotic relationship between Severn and Keats, which the editor highlights by including an "extract from the Preface to 'Adonais,' which Shelley wrote in 1821: . . . 'May the unextinguished spirit of his illustrious friend animate the creations of his [Severn's] pencil, and plead against oblivion for his name!'" (401). The pronoun "his" in the final clause seems to refer to Keats—Shelley wants Severn's pencil to prevent Keats's name from falling into oblivion—but it could very well also refer to Severn (or Shelley or all three). Although Keats's "Ode on a Grecian Urn" and Dickinson's "I died for Beauty –" reveal that "the work, not the poet, is immortal," Shelley's Preface and Severn's article highlight the importance of the poet's fame, whether achieved while living or posthumously, and the dedication of other sympathetic, knowing artists in keeping that name alive.

As Petrino notes, Dickinson's work also reveals the influence of Keats through Barrett Browning. Dickinson most likely read Barrett Browning's "A Vision of Poets" earlier than the 1860s because Sue's copy of *The Poems of Elizabeth Barrett Browning*,[11] which contains "A Vision of Poets," is inscribed "Jan 1st 53." The poem describes Keats as "the real / Adonis, with the hymeneal / Fresh vernal buds half sunk between / His youthful curls, kissed straight and sheen / In his Rome-grave, by Venus queen" (182). Barrett Browning uses imagery Keats himself often used, such as "Fresh vernal buds," which are not yet flowers but carry such beautiful potential. These "buds" refer to nature as well as poetry, and thus Barrett Browning emphasizes Keats's youthfulness and the somewhat wild and unfulfilled qualities of his work, while implying that it is sanctioned ("kissed") by the queen of beauty in classical mythology. Although crowned with these buds in his grave, Keats lives on in Barrett Browning's poem, as do all the other poets she names and describes. The section of "A Vision of Poets" that Petrino sees as echoing Keats and echoed in "I died for Beauty –," which has two pencil markings next to it in Sue's copy, is "These were poets true / Who died for Beauty, as martyrs do / For truth—the ends being scarcely two" (178). The first page of the *Atlantic Monthly* article (September 1861) honoring Barrett

---

[11] See EDR 144, volume 2.

Browning uses her own words to describe her: "[S]he who lived for others was 'poet true, / Who died for Beauty, as martyrs do / For Truth,— the ends being scarcely two.' Beauty *was* truth with her, the wife, mother, and poet, three in one, and such an earthly trinity as God had never before blessed the world with" (368). Barrett Browning is here praised for living "for others" and noted for being a wife and mother before she is described as a poet, but the article ends by aligning her name with other famous artists and thinkers: "Her genius and what she has done for Italy entitle her to companionship with Galileo, Michel Angelo [*sic*], Dante, and Alfieri" (376). Just as Severn's article explores the lasting influence of Keats's name, so too does this article emphasize the importance of Barrett Browning by listing those with whom her name can claim illustrious "companionship."

Sheet Four: Immortal Poets and Sources of Inspiration

I had no Cause to be awake – (Fr662)
I fear a Man of frugal Speech – (Fr663)
Rehearsal to Ourselves (Fr664)
The Martyr Poets – did not tell – (Fr665)

Although Petrino uses the word "martyr" in her discussion of "I died for Beauty," explaining that the poet's death "'for' beauty implies she has died as a martyr in the cause of beauty" (86), the poem itself does not use the word. "Martyr Poets," however, do appear in the last poem of Fascicle 30's fourth sheet, echoing Barrett Browning's lines but collapsing the distinction between those who died for beauty and those who died for truth. "The Martyr Poets – did not tell –" (Fr665) is the most optimistic about the power of art in the fascicle sheets, and it combines Barrett Browning's and Keats's ideas about artistic immortality: artists use their pain to create, and others find solace in that art as well as in the "mortal fate" of the artists. "Poets" and "Painters" toil in silence, "Bequeathing – rather – to their Work – / That when their conscious fingers cease – / Some seek in Art – the Art of Peace –." The poem argues that the poets "wrought their Pang in syllable" and "when their mortal name be numb – / Their mortal fate – encourage Some." The variant for "name" in this line is "fame," revealing Dickinson's concern with the "name" *and* the "fame" of artists, rather than just focusing on the influence of their work. The "mortal name" of the poet lives on and "mortal fame" is not necessarily a prerequisite for the artist to attain artistic immortality. Similarly, the souls of poets live on in their work in Keats's "Bards of Passion and of Mirth," which refrains from mentioning any poets by name, unlike the long list found in "A Vision of Poets." According to Keats, poets "teach us, every day, / Wisdom, though fled far away" (ll. 35–36; page 641 in Dana's collection). Reading poetry is a way to access the divine: "Bards of Passion and of Mirth, / Ye have left your souls on earth! Ye have souls in heaven too, / Double-lived in regions new!" (ll. 39–40). Their work teaches "us, here, the way to find" the poets in heaven (l. 26). These bards "still speak / to mortals," describing their accomplishments as well as their failures: "their sorrows and delights; / Of their passions and their spites; / Of their glory and their shame; / What doth strengthen and what maim" (ll. 30–34). Immortal poetry, then, incorporates the positives and the negatives in order to teach readers wisdom, to tell them "Tales of golden histories / Of heaven and its mysteries" (ll. 21–22).

Several of the poems in Fascicle 30's sheets express ideas related to sorrows, shame, and failure, whereas other poems highlight the power of language and sources of solace and inspiration. The three poems on the same fascicle sheet as "The Martyr Poets," for example, explore the power of language, memory, and sleep. "I fear a Man of frugal speech" (Fr663) emphasizes the power of concision. A "Haranguer" or "Babbler," confesses the poem's speaker, is easily overtaken, but a "Silent Man" who thinks before he speaks is different: "Of this Man – I am wary – / I fear that He is Grand –." "Rehearsal to Ourselves" (Fr664), which follows the "Grand," "frugal" man and precedes "The Martyr Poets," explores the power of memory, particularly of loss or shame. The poem argues that people continue to rehearse "a Withdrawn Delight" because it "Affords a Bliss like Murder." The adjective "Withdrawn" could mean an interior "Delight" that we do not share with others (perhaps because we are ashamed), but it could also mean a "Delight" that has been taken away. "We will not drop the Dirk," or the memory of the delightful/shameful event, "Because We love the Wound." These feelings of pain/shame are so powerful that they become almost enjoyable; they are "Omnipotent – Acute –" and "Remind Us that We died." One way to deal with this pain, as the speaker explains in "The Martyr Poets," is to create art and to "seek in Art – the Art of Peace –." The ideas in these two poems are intertwined in Keats's "Ode to a Nightingale," which presents a speaker so full of heartache that he wishes to "leave this world unseen, / And with thee [the nightingale] fade away into the forest dim" (ll. 19–20; page 54 in Dana's collection). Although Dickinson's speaker views the pain as becoming blissful, Keats's speaker seeks to "quite forget" the "weariness, the fever, and the fret" of human life, which the nightingale "hast never known" (ll. 21–23; page 54). The speaker's suffering and the bird's song envelop him so completely that the poem ends with the speaker wondering, "Was it a vision or a waking dream? / Fled is that music—do I wake or sleep?" (ll. 79–80; page 55). The birdsong, symbolic of poetry, transforms the speaker, perhaps not into happiness but at least to a better understanding of his "sole self" and the timelessness of poetry: "The voice I hear this passing night was heard / In ancient days by emperor and clown" (ll. 72, 63–64; page 55).

In "I had no Cause to be awake –" (Fr662), the poem that begins the fascicle sheet, Dickinson addresses the restorative power of sleep and positive memories. In contrast to Keats's confused speaker in the closing lines of "Ode to a Nightingale," Dickinson's speaker declares "I had no Cause to be awake – / My Best – was gone to sleep – . . . Sweet Morning – When I oversleep – Knock – Recollect – to Me –." The speaker realizes that her "Best," perhaps poetic inspiration, is "gone" when she wakes up, and she asks "Sweet Morning" to remind her. These positive recollections, as we learn in stanzas two and three, are aligned with nature: "I looked at Sunrise – Once – / . . . And wishfulness in me arose – / For Circumstance the same –." The speaker could be remembering the "Sunrise" from her dreams or an actual sunrise that she wants to see well enough in her mind's eye to be inspired by it once again, a feat which she accomplishes in the final stanza: "So choosing but a Gown – / And taking but a Prayer – / . . . I struggled – and was There –." With a little struggle, the speaker returns to the "Ample Peace" held within her memory (or, perhaps, she goes back to sleep). In contrast to "Rehearsal to Ourselves," this poem presents the power of positive memories and the ability to restore oneself through one's own imagination. One can escape the "weariness, the fever, and the fret" of life through imagination, a theme Keats also explores in "Fancy," which argues to "let winged Fancy wander / Through the thought still spread beyond her: / Open wide the mind's cage-door— / She'll dart forth, and cloudward soar" (ll. 5–8; page 111 in Dana's collection). Here, Keats's speaker encourages readers to let Fancy—the wild, somewhat unpredictable little sister of Imagination—fly free, and she will bring you beauty: "She has vassals to attend her; / She will bring, in spite of frost, / Beauties that the earth hath lost" (ll. 28–30; page 111). For Dickinson and for Keats, the positivity of poetic inspiration, whether through dreams, the imagination, or peaceful memories, is often intertwined with nature.

Sheet Five: Poems of Nature and Experience

I cross till I am weary (Fr666)
Answer July – (Fr667)
There is a Shame of Nobleness – (Fr668)

Several scholars have already noted that Dickinson and Keats share a love of nature and incorporate nature's beauty into their work. Diehl, for example, analyzes the similar images in Keats and Dickinson, focusing in particular on some of nature's tiniest objects of beauty that are prevalent in the work of both, such as bees, butterflies, and flowers. Diehl, Mary Loeffelholz, and Virginia Jackson all address the connection between Keats's "The Grasshopper and the

Cricket" and Dickinson's "Further in Summer than the Birds –" (Fr895).[12] Several Dickinson poems have been aligned to Keats's "To Autumn" because they "contain image patterns, especially corn and apples, which harken back to Keats's ode" (Petrino 100 n3). A poem echoing Keats's "To Autumn" that other scholars have not addressed is Dickinson's "Answer July" (Fr667), a poem written on an entire fascicle page without any variants. Dickinson's poem represents an interpretation of the *ubi sunt* ("where are" in Latin) form, which traditionally cues a sense of nostalgia through the use of questions with "gone" as the implied answer. Keats also employs this form in the final stanza of "To Autumn": "Where are the songs of Spring? Ay, where are they? / Think not of them, thou hast thy music too" (ll. 23–24; page 99 in Dana's collection). Although the season of rebirth and renewal is gone, Keats's poem is not nostalgic. Rather, it celebrates loss and understands the integral role that the "stubble-plains" (l. 26) of autumn play in the unalterable cycle of seasons. Dickinson's version of the *ubi sunt* takes up Keats's celebration of loss but focuses on the cyclical movement of seasons to articulate a comfort that can be found within this fact of nature and life on earth. In Dickinson's poem, certain seasons ask where other seasons have gone, and the stanzas change as the questioned seasons reply. Dickinson's poem represents the fluidity of the seasons, and the grammatical fluidity that closes the first stanza of "To Autumn" reflects a similar movement. The fluidity in Dickinson's poem ends with a sense of containment. Despite the questioning and answering of different months, the poem answers that they are all contained "Here –" within "the Year –."[13] Keats's "To Autumn" celebrates death because the transience makes nature and human life beautiful, but "To Autumn" also offers "a philosophical understanding that this is the only real world we have" (Stillinger 477), and Dickinson poignantly translates this in her *ubi sunt*. The seasons are only and always "Here" on earth; "the Year," despite all the fluctuations that will occur in one's life as time passes, will always contain those seasons and the familiar emblems of each, such as the "Bee," "Bud," "Snow," and "Maise." Dickinson translates Keats's flowery, often enjambed lines into concise

---

[12] Virginia Jackson's discussion of the manuscript history of "Further in Summer than the Birds –" exemplifies her argument that the history of lyric reading has transformed our understanding of Dickinson's texts; see pages 68–100.

[13] Dickinson's emphasis on "the Year" could be an echo of Percy Shelley's poem about autumn, which follows Keats's ode in the Dana collection that Dickinson could have read. In contrast to Keats's poem, which does not use the word "year," Shelley describes autumn as the time when "the Year" is on her "death-bed" (l. 4). He mentions "the Year" twice in the poem and also twice uses the phrase "the dead, cold Year." Dickinson's poem, however, emphasizes the comforting reliability and movement of the seasons within "the Year," in contrast to Shelley's contention that autumn represents the year's death.

statements, and the two poems share several similar images. Dickinson uses "Blush" instead of the "rosy hue" of the "stubble-plains" in Keats; instead of the "sweet kernel[s]" of corn, Dickinson refers to "Maise" (her misspelling of "maize") to rhyme with "Haze," which harkens back to the opening line of Keats's poem: "Season of mist and mellow fruitfulness!"

Seeking solace and inspiration in nature and poetry is a theme throughout Keats and the Fascicle 30 sheets. Neither poet, however, ignores the power of negative emotions, particularly self-doubt. "Answer July," for example, is couched between two poems that explore the effects of secret shame and mental exhaustion. "There is a Shame of Nobleness" (Fr668), which follows "Answer July" and closes the fascicle sheet, explores "Confronting" a secret "Shame," such as acquiring "Sudden Pelf." According to Dickinson's *Webster*, "pelf" refers to "riches; but it often conveys something ill gotten or worthless."[14] The second stanza gives the example of the "best Disgrace" that "a Brave Man feels" when "Acknowledged – of the Brave;" a feeling of disgrace seems out of place, unless only he knows that he is not truly brave. The poem's diction reveals the paradox of secret knowledge, describing it as a "Shame of Extasy" because it is "Convicted of Itself." The shame stemming from this self-doubt and self-knowledge, most likely hidden from others, becomes almost pleasant. The self-doubt in the fascicle sheet's first poem, however, brings only weariness and confusion. The speaker explains the feeling of mental exhaustion: "I cross till I am weary / A Mountain – in my mind –" (Fr666). Despite a lengthy journey, the speaker's "Pace" is not "defeat[ed]," until "the Grace [is] in sight – / I shout unto my feet – / . . . They strive – and yet delay." Once "Heaven" is in view—the speaker so close to "the Goal," although the poem never specifies what that goal is—the speaker cannot get any closer, and she eventually fails: "Do we die – / Or is this Death's experiment – / Reversed – in Victory?"

Sheet Six: The Power of Pain

An ignorance a Sunset (Fr669)
One Crucifixion is recorded – only – (Fr670)
The Sweetest Heresy received (Fr671)
Take Your Heaven further on – (Fr672)

The failure of the mental journey feels like death or some strange victory akin to death, and the solution to this weary confusion is found in the reliability of nature in "Answer July," which follows "There is a Shame of Nobleness." In contrast to "I cross till I am weary," which ends with a speaker questioning whether a victory

---

[14] See http://edl.byu.edu/webster/p/52.

has occurred, the first poem of the sixth sheet expresses confidence in victory: the final stanza states that "when the solemn features" of human faces "Confirm – in Victory – / We start – as if detected / In Immortality –." This poem opens with the idea that "An ignorance a Sunset / Confer upon the Eye –" (Fr669). In contrast to the comfort or inspiration one can often find in nature, as other poems in the fascicle sheets suggest, this poem articulates the inferiority of humans in the face of nature's—and, by extension, heaven's—glory. Sunset's "Amber Revelation" is exhilarating and debasing because when we are inspected by "Omnipotence," we are found "inferior." And yet there is a sense of "Victory" in that inferiority, which is so surprising that it startles us so powerfully that it feels like we have suddenly been discovered "In Immortality." The sheet's second poem continues to explore ideas of human suffering, recognizing that "Our Lord – indeed – made Compound Witness," yet humans have within them the potential for pain "in the Being's Centre" that is reminiscent of the place where Christ was crucified. In "One Crucifixion is recorded – only –" (Fr670), the speaker knows that crucifixions other than Christ's have occurred: "How many be / Is not affirmed of Mathematics – / Or History –." One cannot find records of these other crucifixions, yet the speaker knows "There's newer – nearer Crucifixion / Than That –."

These final lines of "One Crucifixion" spill over onto the next page of the fascicle sheet, which contains "The Sweetest Heresy received" (Fr671), allowing the poem's final claim about crucifixions to be quickly appeased by a "Faith" that can "accommodate but Two." Karl Keller reads "The Sweetest Heresy received" as Dickinson's agreement with "the Puritan arrangements for man and woman," where marriage is "a sufficient religion" (27). The poem argues that "The Ritual" of marriage is "so small" and "The Grace so unavoidable" that "To fail – is Infidel –." "The Sweetest Heresy received" is a succinct argument in two stanzas with no variants, and the poem's commanding concision seems to support Keller's conclusion. However, the final poem on this fascicle sheet complicates the prior security in "Puritan arrangements." The speaker in "Take Your Heaven further on –" (Fr672) may also be getting married since "Dressed to meet You – / See – in White!" evokes the image of a bride. This bride, however, is a "Sufferer polite," and she seems to be speaking from beyond the grave: "This – to Heaven divine Has gone – / Had You earlier blundered in / Possibly, e'en You had seen / An Eternity – put on –." The "Sufferer polite" could be a woman who waited for her suitor to "blunder in" and propose marriage to her. However, he arrives too late and she has already gone "to Heaven divine." For the man left behind, "to ring a Door beyond / Is the utmost of Your Hand –." The "Sufferer polite" commands him to "apologize" "To the Skies," rather than to her, because the sky is "Nearer to Your Courtesies." In print, "Take Your Heaven further on –" is normally presented as a single stanza, indicating a fluid, almost breathless exasperation aimed at the one the speaker has left behind. In the manuscript, however, three single words are set off on lines of their own: "in," "beyond," and "Hand –." The effect remains one of vexation, but there is such little blank space on the sheet that the three relatively small gaps created by these single-word lines indicate a visual pause before "Possibly," "Is the utmost," and "To the Skies." These gaps allow one to envision an overwhelmed speaker who needs a moment to catch her breath. The pause before "Possibly" also highlights the speaker's uncertainty that "Had You earlier blundered in" "e'en You" would have "seen / An Eternity – put on –."

Because "Dressed" "in White" likely evokes a bride for many readers, it is easy to read this poem as about marriage; it does, after all, follow "The Sweetest Heresy received." But it could also be about literary aspirations. In *Aurora Leigh*, for example, Aurora's cousin, Romney, finds her book and tells her: "'Ah, / But men, and still less women, happily, / Scarce need be poets. Keep to the green wreath, / Since even dreaming of the stone and bronze / Brings headaches, pretty cousin, and defiles / The clean white morning dresses'" (ll. 2.91–96; page 42).[15] Here, "white morning dresses" have nothing to do with marriage, but they are defiled by a woman doing something so unfeminine as writing poetry. The speaker as a "Sufferer polite – / Dressed to meet You – / See – in White!" could be a reference to Aurora, who is struggling to be a "Woman and artist" (l. 2.4; page 40), as well as an allusion to Barrett Browning and Dickinson, who also struggle "in this twofold sphere" where "still the artist is intensely a man" (ll. 7.777–778; page 274).[16] In an 1873 letter to her Norcross cousins, in fact, Dickinson adapts the idea in 1 Corinthians 15:53[17] to show how she feels about George Eliot's writing: "'What do I think of *Middlemarch*?' What do I think of glory—except that in a few instances, this 'mortal has already put on immortality.' George Eliot is one" (L389). According to Dickinson's view in this letter, a mortal writer can "put on immortality" and achieve glory on earth, although this does not happen often. In a very subtle, interesting way, then, this poem that seems at first to be about a spurned woman returns to the theme of artistic immortality. The poem's speaker has successfully donned "Eternity" through her work,

---

[15] A later reference in *Aurora Leigh* does connect the white dress with a yearning for marriage: "'There? Dear, you are asleep still; don't you know / The five Miss Granvilles? always dressed in white / To show they're ready to be married'" (ll. 4.634–636; page 143).
[16] Pencil markings exist next to many of the lines on this page in Sue's copy; see EDR 197.
[17] "For the trumpet shall sound, and the dead shall be raised incorruptible, and we shall be changed. For this corruptible must put on incorruption, and this mortal must put on immortality. So when this corruptible shall have put on incorruption, and this mortal shall shave put on immortality, then shall be brought to pass the saying that is written, Death is swallowed up in victory" (1 Corinthians 15:52–54).

perhaps having "left her soul on earth" with a soul "in heaven too," as in Keats's "Bards of Passion and of Mirth" (ll. 2–3).

Sheet One: Nature's Ephemeral Beauty

No Crowd that has occurred (Fr653)
Beauty – be not caused – It is – (Fr654)
He parts Himself – like Leaves – (Fr655)

In contrast to the concern in "One Crucifixion" of the "newer – nearer" crucifixions, the poem that opens the first fascicle sheet expresses awe at another event centered on Christ: "No Crowd that has occurred / Exhibit – I suppose / The General Attendance / That Resurrection does –" (Fr653). The event is so miraculous that "All Multitudes that were / [are] Efface[d] in the Comparison." The witnesses in the "Crowd" are "August – Absorbed – Numb –." The speaker concludes by wondering what other event (what "Duplicate – exist[s]") could hold such a "Significance" as "This – / To Universe – and Me?" One possible answer to this question is found in the poem that follows it: "Beauty – be not caused – It is –" (Fr654), a declarative statement that Dickinson would later translate in "Further in Summer than the Birds –" (Fr895A) as "Beauty – is Nature's Fact –." This "Beauty" exists without human interference and is evidence of heaven's glory on earth. In *Emily Dickinson's Poems: As She Preserved Them*, Cristanne Miller notes that the opening line of Fr654 refers to Ralph Waldo Emerson's idea in "The Rhodora" that "beauty is its own excuse for being" (763 n266). Dickinson's poem argues that this beauty only "abides" when one does not "Chase it." If you decide to "Chase it," then "it ceases." In other words, a witness of nature's gifts should appreciate them without trying to pursue or control them. The poem's example of this beauty—and why chasing it is pointless—is "when the Wind / Runs his fingers" through "the Meadow," explaining that "Deity will see to it" that you never "Overtake the Creases." Keats's "Nature and the Poets" expresses a similar observation that interacting with beauty, rather than merely observing it, can cause it to disappear. Keats's speaker observes the beauty of "swarms of minnows" in a stream, noting that "If you but scantily hold out the hand, / That very instant not one will remain; / But turn your eye, and they are there again" (ll. 72, 78–80; page 50 in Dana's collection).

This first fascicle sheet ends with "He parts Himself – like Leaves –" (Fr655), a poem that intertwines the inevitability of death with nature's beauty. As in Keats's work and other Fascicle 30 poems, this poem explores the solace one can find in nature, symbolized by the butterfly, while acknowledging that all life eventually comes to an end. Dickinson's poem records the actions of a butterfly, at first realistically and then in such a way that the butterfly becomes supernatural: "He parts Himself – like Leaves – / . . . Then stands upon the Bonnet / Of Any Buttercup – / . . . And dangles like a Mote . . . Uncertain – to return Below – / Or settle in the Moon –." The apparent magical abilities of this butterfly recall the magic of Keats's nightingale: "The same [song] that oft-times hath / Charm'd magic casements, opening on the foam / Of perilous seas, in faery lands forlorn" (ll. 68–70). The vision of the butterfly is what inspires Dickinson's poem, whereas Keats's poem relies upon the nightingale's song. Both, however, track the movement and song of nature's creatures beyond normal human capabilities. The final stanza reminds us that everything, including the butterfly, must die: "The Frost – possess the World – / . . . A Sepulchre of quaintest Floss – / An Abbey – a Cocoon –." The transition from a "Sepulchre" to a "Cocoon"—from grave to a place of rebirth—provides some comfort, however: the cycle of life continues, for butterflies and humans alike.

Sheet Two: Poetic Inspiration and the Power of Language

I started Early – Took my Dog – (Fr656)
"Morning" – means "Milking" – to the Farmer – (Fr191B)
Endow the Living – with the Tears – (Fr657B)

The second fascicle sheet opens with "I started Early – Took my Dog –" (Fr656), a poem that has been read in a number of ways, most of which involve sex, fear, or both.[18] Carrie O'Maley, for example, claims critics agree that the poem's "main theme . . . is the male/female sexual encounter," although O'Maley states "the encounter is with death" (86, 87). Jonnie Guerra, in contrast, finds "a far more lighthearted interpretation of the poem's erotic encounter" (78). I read this poem in its fascicle context as a dream, one which involves poetic inspiration, largely because the poem Dickinson placed after it begins with "Morning." The speaker in "I started Early" mentions that "no Man moved Me

---

[18] Kate Flores suggests "it is a study in fear, fear of love, of which the sea is here the symbol" (87). Eric Carlson sees the poem as "a dramatization of the frightening realization that toying with love may arouse a tide of emotion too powerful to control" (137). In *A Poet's Grammar,* Cristanne Miller writes that "The speaker's tale becomes a sexual fantasy— repeated either in her imagining of what it would be like to walk by what she sees as a masculine and therefore dangerous sea, or in her imagination as she in fact walks by the sea, or in her metaphorical representation of real dealings with the world of men" (74). Susan Anderson reads the poem in terms of power relations: "The mouse as persona in poem 520 [Fr656], though, does not derive from the female speaker's own identification with the figure but from other figures in the poem who assume that she is a mouse. This speaker's perceived insignificance, however, becomes her means to power. Those who believe she is a mouse naturally assume her to be mousy, but she proves these presumptions false" (90).

– till the Tide / Went past my simple Shoe – / . . . I felt His Silver Heel / Opon my Ancle – Then My Shoes / Would overflow with Pearl –." Dickinson refers in a few letters to her books as pearls,[19] and overflowing "with Pearl" in the poem could be read as creative inspiration within the dream. Cristanne Miller observes, "The sudden introduction of the conditional 'Would'" implies that "what seemed a single action in the past now seems to be either a hypothetical or a customary, repeated action" (74). Although Miller does not read the poem as a dream or as literary inspiration, her observation that the "overflow" of "Pearl" could be a "repeated action" coincides with creative influence. Dickinson's elegies reflect her close association with female authors, and the claim that "no Man moved Me" could refer to inspiration gained from women writers.[20] The sensual dream of a visit to the sea could have led to a "Morning" filled with poetic inspiration. Although Keats does not use a pearl to symbolize literary inspiration, both Keats and Shakespeare associate morning with pearls of dew. In Dana's collection, for example, Shakespeare's "Song of the Fairy" ends with the fairy saying, "I must go seek some dewdrops here / And hang a pearl in every cowslip's ear" (ll. 13–14; page 529). Shakespeare finds poetic inspiration in the natural beauty of morning, associating that beauty with the magical work fairies perform at night. Shakespeare's poem is followed by Keats's homage to these fairies in "Fairy Song": "Shed no tear! O shed no tear! / The flower will bloom another year" (ll. 1–2; page 529). The fairy's song seeks to soothe the cares of humans by drawing their attention to the beauty and reliability of nature. The "Silver Heel" of the sea touches the ankle of Dickinson's speaker, and the "silvery bill" of Keats's fairy "Ever cures the good man's ill" (ll. 13–14; page 529). In "Fancy," Keats describes how one can find leaves and flowers "Pearled" with dew on a spring morning; this vision is one in a long list of spring's beauties, brought to the speaker by "Fancy": "She will bring thee, all together, / . . . All the buds and bells of May" (ll. 54, 31–33; page 111).

The connection between sensuality and poetry is also found in Keats, who describes Endymion, the beautiful shepherd who falls in love with the moon goddess, in "Nature and the Poets" as "a Poet, sure a lover too" (l. 193; page 52). In addition, while the poem's speaker wanders alone to record nature's beauty, he takes a moment to wish that he will happen upon a beautiful woman also enjoying nature: "How she would start and blush, thus to be caught / Playing in all her innocence of thought! / O let me lead her gently o'er the brook, / Watch her half-smiling lips and downward look" (ll. 99–102; pages 50–51). According

---

[19] L162: "I look in my casket and miss a pearl –." Johnson sees the line as perhaps "a reminder that Emmons still has not returned the book which ED lent him" (295).
[20] Dickinson wrote three elegies for Elizabeth Barrett Browning, one for George Eliot, and one for Charlotte Bronte, and refers to Emily Bronte as "gigantic" (L267).

to the poem, we know the stories of classic myths largely because the "bard[s] of old" "pulled the boughs aside, / That we might look into a forest wide, / To catch a glimpse of Fauns, and Dryades" (ll. 163, 151–153; page 51). These bards often sung of sensuality and suffering, such as the story of Psyche and Love and "how they kist each other's tremulous eyes ... the ravishment—the wonder— / The darkness—loneliness—the fearful thunder" (ll. 146–148; page 51). In "Fancy," Keats's speaker encourages readers to let their "Fancy" be as wild and as pure as before the trials of life altered it (and them): "Dulcet-eyed as Ceres' daughter / Ere the god of Torment taught her / How to frown and how to chide; With a waist and with a side / White as Hebe's, when her zone / Slipt its golden clasp, and down / Fell her kirtle to her feet, / While she held the goblet sweet" (ll. 81–88; pages 111–112). Hebe was the daughter of Jupiter and Juno and served as cupbearer to the gods, until a wardrobe malfunction exposed her, which led to Jupiter replacing her with the boy Ganymede.

"I started Early" takes up both sides of the first leaf of the folded fascicle page; when opened, the fascicle sheet displays the end of the dream on the left, and we find on the right, in two neat, distinct stanzas with no variants, "'Morning' – means 'Milking' – to the Farmer –" (Fr191B). In his 1998 edition, Franklin notes that a variant of Fr191 was sent to Sue about 1861 and then copied into Fascicle 30 about 1863: "Although two years apart, the copies probably derived from the same draft, now destroyed" (224–225). The earlier version sent to Sue proves Dickinson copied this poem into the fascicle for a purpose, which I see as highlighting the power of language and supporting the reading of "I started Early" as a dream. The poem explains how the significance of "Morning" alters according to the person and the situation. The first stanza centers on meaning, such as morning means "Dice – to the Maid –," and the second stanza highlights time, as in the "Epicures – date a Breakfast – by it –." What is surprising, especially following a rather mundane opening about "Morning" meaning work, is that "Morning means just Risk – to the Lover – / Just Revelation to the Beloved –." Dickinson's inclusion here of a cheating couple could indicate that a "Lover" being revealed to "the Beloved" is a common occurrence; that the revealing light of "Morning" provides the "Risk" and the excitement for one and the heartbreak for the other. "I started Early" presents a dream world imbued with eroticism, and this poem highlights the "Risk" of marriage, or of being "the *wife forgotten*" (L93), which could explain why "Morning" represents "an Apocalypse" for "Brides."

"'Morning' – means 'Milking'" appears at first only to investigate "Morning." The closing line, however, comments on "Faith," which, according to the formula of the second stanza, dates "The Experiment of Our Lord –" by morning. How to interpret this line represents a difficulty: what is "The Experiment of Our Lord," and how does "Faith" date this "Experiment" by morning? Perhaps human existence is the experiment; thus, "Faith" dates life by morning and "Faith" is measured through the succession of mornings, the passing by of life. The final line's postulation of how faith and life are related to morning could be a reference to the endless movement of time—no matter what happens to humans, or no matter what those on earth experience during this "Experiment," morning will always arrive. The possibility of endless tomorrows, with night the only reprieve "from Sighing" for those experiencing "Faint-going lives," reveals a fact of nature (the sun will always rise tomorrow) that *can* be comforting but may be arduously banal. In contrast, the next poem (the last on this fascicle sheet) tries to teach a lesson based on life's unpredictability. The poem demands that readers make the most of the time they have on earth with the people they love: "Endow the Living – with the Tears – / You squander on the Dead" (Fr657B). If we take those who are alive for granted, then they will "deny" the "Cherishing" we give them after they have died. Life's unpredictability, rather than being a source of despair and fear, should force us to value the "Men and Women" in front of us.

Sheet Three: The Power of Failure

> 'Tis true – They shut me in the Cold – (Fr658)
> The Province of the Saved (Fr659)
> I took my Power in my Hand – (Fr660)
> Some such Butterfly be seen (Fr661)

The third fascicle sheet continues to explore human failure and suffering. The opening poem, "'Tis true – They shut me in the Cold –" (Fr658), explores a self in isolation from others, yet the speaker can withstand the pain of that isolation as well as forgive the ones who caused the "Harm." In contrast to the speaker "in the Cold," "Themselves were warm / And could not know the feeling 'twas –." The speaker asks the "Lord" to "Forget it" and to "Let not my Witness hinder Them / In Heavenly esteem –." The final stanza demands that Christ "Forgive them" because the speaker, the one "who bore it," has already done so. The speaker can be so forgiving, and ordering Christ to be forgiving as well, because she realizes the difficulty of understanding a situation one has not experienced. Inside, warm, and together, "They" "could not know the feeling" of the "Cold." This exploration of the power of negative experiences harkens back to Keats's "Bards of Passion and of Mirth," where poets "teach us, every day, / Wisdom, though fled far away" (ll. 35–36; page 641 in Dana's collection). The immortal poets do not write only about their glory but about their "sorrows," "spites," and "shame." In the next poem, Dickinson portrays the wisdom gained from these negative experiences as a form of art: "The Province of the Saved / Should be the Art – To save –" (Fr659). The opening stanza argues that those who are

"Saved" should be the ones to save others, and this process is an "Art" as well as a "Science." Those who understand "The Science of the Grave" should turn this knowledge into an "Art – To save" others. Only a "Man" who understands suffering is "qualified / To qualify Despair," and those who do not understand will "Mistake Defeat for Death – Each time."

However, sometimes one's "Power" simply fails, resulting in confusion rather than in wisdom or understanding, which is one way of reading Dickinson's "I took my Power in my Hand –" (Fr660). When the fascicle sheet is open, one finds "The Province of the Saved" on the left and "I took my Power in my Hand –" on the right. Both use images from Christian discourse and both explore "Defeat," yet the bold speaker on the right uses an unnamed "Power" to go "against the World," which contrasts with the specific "Art – to save" on the left. Read in isolation, the poem is typically associated with Dickinson's poetic aspirations: "I aimed my Pebble – but Myself / Was all the one that fell – / Was it Goliah – was too large – / Or was myself – too small?"[21] The "Power" need not be specific to poetry, however; it could refer to the power of any person who seeks to take on a "Goliah." Sometimes, for reasons we do not understand, the world just wins. But nature remains to console us. The poem that closes this fascicle sheet again observes a butterfly, whether real or imaginary: "Some such Butterfly be seen / On Brazilian Pampas –." The experience is fleeting, as is the scent of a flower in the second stanza: "Some such Spice – express – and pass – / Subject to your plucking –." The speaker's familiarity with (and then loss of) the butterfly and flower is compared to "the Stars," which you can only know at "Night;" by "Morning," they are "Foreigners." Although the Fascicle 30 poems recognize the "weariness, the fever, and the fret" of life, the solace of nature and imagination remains integral, just as Keats's speaker in "Nature and the Poets" describes: "So I straightway began to pluck a posy, / Of luxuries bright, milky, soft, and rosy: / A bush of May-flowers with the bees about them; / Ah, sure no tasteful nook could be without them!" (ll. 27–30; page 50). The pun of posy/poesy collapses the distinction between the power of poems and nature's emblems of beauty, an aspect of Keats that Dickinson clearly appreciated.

Conclusion

The sheets of Fascicle 30 reveal a specific, clear correlation between the themes explored by John Keats and Emily Dickinson. Other than in "I died for Beauty," Dickinson does not directly quote Keats, a form of homage she did not widely

---

[21] Jack Capps, for example, writes that in "I took my Power in my Hand," Dickinson "uses the story of David and Goliath to warn against ill-considered aspirations, and, in the role of David, Emily loses" (38–39).

use in her poems;[22] instead, she gathered aspects of his language, his images and symbols, and translated them to suit her own means and style. Locating the Keatsian echoes in the fascicle provides a deeper understanding of how Dickinson understood the work and life of a poet. We also achieve a better understanding of Keats through Dickinson's translations of him and by tracing the complicated layers of influence through which texts inspire the textual production of poets and writers across time and space. The connections and contrasts wrought by language reveal why—for artists and audiences—"Some seek in Art – the Art of Peace –."

Works Cited

The following abbreviations are used to refer to the writings of Emily Dickinson:

    Fr   *The Poems of Emily Dickinson*, edited by R. W. Franklin, Harvard UP, 1998. Citation by poem number.

    L   *The Letters of Emily Dickinson*, edited by Thomas H. Johnson and Theodora Ward, Harvard UP, 1958. Citation by letter number.

Anderson, Susan M. "'Regard[ing] a Mouse' in Dickinson's Poems and Letters." *The Emily Dickinson Journal*, vol. 2, no. 1, 1993, pp. 84–102.

Browning, Elizabeth Barrett. *Aurora Leigh*. C. S. Francis & Co., 1857.

----. "A Vision of Poets." *The Poems of Elizabeth Barrett Browning*, C. S. Francis & Co., 1852, pp. 167–204.

Cameron, Sharon. *Choosing Not Choosing: Dickinson's Fascicles*. U of Chicago P, 1992.

Capps, Jack. *Emily Dickinson's Reading: 1836-1886*. Harvard UP, 1966.

Carlson, Eric W. "Dickinson's 'I started Early – Took my Dog.'" *Explicator*, vol. 20, no. 9, 1962, pp. 136–139.

Chambers, Robert, ed. *Cyclopaedia of English Literature*, vol. II, William and Robert Chambers, 1844.

Crumbley, Paul and Eleanor Elson Heginbotham, eds. *Dickinson's Fascicles: A Spectrum of Possibilities*. The Ohio State UP, 2014.

Dana, Charles A., ed. *The Household Book of Poetry*. D. Appleton and Company, 1860.

Dickinson, Emily. *Emily Dickinson's Poems: As She Preserved Them*, edited by Cristanne Miller, Belknap Press of Harvard UP, 2016.

----. *The Manuscript Books of Emily Dickinson*, edited by R. W. Franklin, Belknap Press of Harvard UP, 1981.

---

[22] Elizabeth Petrino explains, "Vivian Pollack notes that about fifty-one poems contain direct quotation" (82). For more details about how Dickinson used direct quotation, see Cynthia Hallen's essay in this collection.

Diehl, Joanne Feit. *Dickinson and the Romantic Imagination*. Princeton UP, 1981.

"Elizabeth Barrett Browning." *The Atlantic Monthly*, vol. 8, September 1861, pp. 368–376.

Emily Dickinson Lexicon website, Brigham Young University, 2007, http://edl.byu.edu/index.php.

Farr, Judith. *The Passion of Emily Dickinson*. Harvard UP, 1992.

Flores, Kate. "Dickinson's 'I started Early – Took my Dog.'" *Explicator*, vol. 9, no. 7, 1951, pp. 86–89.

Franklin, R. W. Introduction. *The Poems of Emily Dickinson*. 3 vols. Belknap Press of Harvard UP, 1998, pp. i–vii.

Guerra, Jonnie G. "Dickinson's 'I started Early – Took my Dog.'" *Explicator*, vol. 50, no. 2, Winter 1992, pp. 78–80.

Heginbotham, Eleanor. *Reading the Fascicles of Emily Dickinson: Dwelling in Possibilities*. Ohio UP, 2003.

Higginson, T. W. "Letter to a Young Contributor." *The Atlantic Monthly*, vol. 9, no. 54, April 1862, pp. 401–411.

----. "The Life of Birds." *The Atlantic Monthly*, vol. 10, no. 59, September 1862, pp. 368–377.

Jackson, Virginia. *Dickinson's Misery: A Theory of Lyric Reading*. Princeton UP, 2005.

Keats, John. *Complete Poems*, edited by Jack Stillinger, Harvard UP, 1982.

Keller, Karl. *The Only Kangaroo among the Beauty: Emily Dickinson and America*. Johns Hopkins UP, 1979.

Miller, Cristanne. *A Poet's Grammar*. Harvard UP, 1987.

Miller, Ruth. *The Poetry of Emily Dickinson*. Wesleyan UP, 1968.

O'Maley, Carrie. "Dickinson's 'I started Early – Took my Dog.'" *Explicator*, vol. 60, no. 2, Winter 2003, pp. 86–88.

Petrino, Elizabeth. "Allusion, Echo, and Literary Influence in Emily Dickinson." *The Emily Dickinson Journal*, vol. 19, no. 1, 2010, pp. 80–102.

Severn, Joseph. "On the Vicissitudes of Keats's Fame." *The Atlantic Monthly*, vol. 11, no. 66, April 1863, pp. 401–407.

Socarides, Alexandra. *Dickinson Unbound: Paper, Process, Poetics*. Oxford UP, 2012.

----. "Dickinson, Higginson, and the Problem with Print." Philadelphia, PA: Society for the Study of American Women Writers conference, 25 October 2009.

----. "Rethinking the Fascicles: Dickinson's Writing, Copying, and Binding Practices." *The Emily Dickinson Journal*, vol. 15, no. 2, 2006, pp. 69–94.

Swyderski, Ann. "Dickinson's Enchantment: the Barrett Browning Fascicles." *Symbiosis: A Journal of Anglo-American Literary Relations*, vol. 7, no.1, April 2003, pp. 76–98.

Wardrop, Daneen. "Emily Dickinson and the Gothic in Fascicle 16." *The Cambridge Companion to Emily Dickinson*, edited by Wendy Martin, Cambridge UP, 2002, pp. 142–164.

Webster, Noah. *An American Dictionary of the English Language.* 2 vol. reprint of the 1841 edition, Adams Brothers, 1844. Online renovated edition at http://edl.byu.edu/webster.

Wohlpart, James A. "A New Redemption: Emily Dickinson's Poetic in Fascicle 22 and 'I Dwell in Possibility.'" *South Atlantic Review,* vol. 66, no. 1, Winter 2001, pp. 50–83.

Further Reading

Brantley, Richard. *Experience and Faith: The Late-Romantic Imagination of Emily Dickinson.* Palgrave Macmillan, 2004.

Bray, Robert. "Why Thoughts Are Better Than Music or Emily Dickinson's Fascicle 18 as a Lyric Sequence." Modern Language Association roundtable, 30 December 1997, http://archive.emilydickinson.org/fascicle/bray.html.

Cambon, Glauco. "Emily Dickinson and the Crisis of Self-Reliance." *Transcendentalism and Its Legacy,* edited by Myron Simon and Thornton H. Parsons, U of Michigan P, 1966.

Carton, Evan. *The Rhetoric of American Romance: Dialectic and Identity in Emerson, Dickinson, Poe, and Hawthorne.* Johns Hopkins UP, 1985.

Diehl, Joanne Feit. *Women Poets and the American Sublime.* Indiana UP, 1990.

Doreski, William. "'An Exchange of Territory': Dickinson's Fascicle 27." *ESQ: A Journal of the American Renaissance,* vol. 32, no. 1, 1986, pp. 55–67.

Gribbin, Laura. "Emily Dickinson's Circumference: Figuring a Blind Spot in the Romantic Tradition." *The Emily Dickinson Journal,* vol. 2, no. 1, 1993, pp. 1–22.

Oberhaus, Dorothy Huff. *Emily Dickinson's Fascicles: Method & Meaning.* Pennsylvania State UP, 1995.

Rosenthal, M. L. and Sally M. Gall. *The Modern Poetic Sequence: The Genius of Modern Poetry.* Oxford UP, 1983.

Shurr, William. *The Marriage of Emily Dickinson.* Kentucky UP, 1983.

Wolosky, Shira. "Dickinson's Emerson: A Critique of American Identity." *The Emily Dickinson Journal,* vol. 9, no. 2, 2000, pp. 134–141.

Index

2

2Pac, 101, 102, 104, 105, 107, 108, 109, 110, 111, 112, 113, 114, 116, 117, 118

A

Ackmann, Martha, vii, 102, 109, 111, 117
afterlife, ix, 102, 103, 104, 105, 113, 115
allusions, 2, 3, 11, 15, 129
Amaral, Ana Luísa, 67, 98
Amherst Academy, 2, 4, 13, 62, 69, 77, 79
analogy, 3
Anderson, Susan M., 140, 145

B

Baker, James V., 92, 98
Balmer, Paul, 95, 98
Becker, Alton, 7, 61
belief, 6, 7, 103, 106, 124, 129
bells, 88, 93, 141
Bennett, Fordyce R., 3
Bennett, Paula, 62, 103, 117
Benvenuto, Richard, 4, 62
Bianchi, Martha Dickinson, 4, 10, 61, 69, 95, 98
Bible, 7, 12, 62, 122
Biblical, 2, 3, 11, 12
Bingham, Millicent Todd, 76, 98
birdsong, 47, 50, 86, 88, 92, 133
Boxall, Peter, 115, 117
Boziwick, George, 79, 94, 96, 98

Brantley, Richard, 127, 147
Brashear, Lucy, 9, 10, 61
Bray, Robert, 124, 147
Browning, Elizabeth Barrett, 74, 93, 123, 127, 129, 130, 131, 132, 138, 141, 145, 146
Buckingham, Willis, 4, 62
Budick, E. Miller, 3, 62
Burbick, Joan, 3, 62

C

Calvinism, 70, 80, 103, 107, 117
Cambon, Glauco, 127, 147
Cameron, Sharon, 124, 145
Capps, Jack, 144, 145
Carlson, Eric W., 140, 145
Carton, Evan, 127, 147
Cato, 11, 13
Chambers, Robert, 15, 99, 128, 145
Child, Lydia Maria, 47, 75, 98
Christ, 12, 15, 16, 18, 39, 47, 52, 53, 102, 104, 122, 137, 139, 143
Christianity, 102, 104, 107
Civil War, 87, 109, 111
collocation, 3, 5
Crumbley, Paul, 62, 95, 98, 124, 145
Cuddy, Lois A., 3, 62

D

Dana, Charles, 128, 132, 133, 134, 135, 139, 141, 143, 145
death, ix, 4, 6, 8, 9, 10, 15, 18, 22, 47, 48, 49, 70, 86, 87, 88, 89, 90, 92, 93, 101, 104, 105, 106, 111,

112, 113, 114, 115, 116, 117, 118,
  127, 129, 132, 135, 136, 138, 139,
  140, 144
Dickinson, Austin, 4, 11, 35, 76, 78,
  95, 111, 122, 128
Dickinson, Edward, 4, 13, 71
Diehl, Joanne Feit, 127, 134, 146,
  147
direct quotation, ix, 2, 145
Dobson, Joanne, 108, 117
Doreski, William, 124, 147
dream, 48, 133, 140, 142
drum, 86, 87, 88
Dyson, Michael Eric, 107, 117

E

Eberwein, Jane Donahue, 4, 61, 99,
  103, 107, 111, 117, 118
Edwards, Walter, 111, 112, 113, 117
Ellis, Aimé J., 109, 117
Emerson, Ralph Waldo, 18, 102,
  127, 129, 139, 147
Emily Dickinson Lexicon, ix, 2, 14,
  15, 17, 61, 90, 99, 146
England, Martha Winburn, 71, 74,
  99

F

Farr, Judith, 117, 118, 121, 122, 146
fascicles, vii, x, 3, 62, 79, 119, 120,
  121, 122, 123, 124, 125, 126, 128,
  129, 130, 132, 133, 134, 135, 136,
  137, 139, 140, 142, 143, 144, 145,
  146, 147
fingering, 82
Flores, Kate, 140, 146
Franklin, R. W., 10, 19, 38, 47, 51,
  61, 88, 98, 116, 120, 121, 122,
  123, 124, 125, 126, 130, 142, 145,
  146

Freeman, Margaret H., 3, 62
Fuss, Diana, 75, 99

G

Gall, Sally M., 124, 147
gangsta rap, 104, 105, 106, 107,
  108, 112, 113, 114, 115, 116
Garland, Roland, 4, 62
Gilbert, Sandra M., 100, 104, 111,
  117, 121, 128
God, 5, 6, 7, 8, 9, 10, 12, 13, 15, 24,
  47, 48, 51, 52, 71, 91, 102, 103,
  104, 105, 106, 107, 115, 116, 117,
  118, 132
Gribbin, Laura, 127, 147
Guerra, Jonnie G., 140, 146
guns, 107, 108, 110, 115, 118
Gura, Philip F., 1, 61

H

Hagenbüchle, Roland, 3, 62, 117
Hamilton, Craig, 3, 62
Hart, Ellen Louise, 67, 99
Hasse, John E., 94, 99
Heginbotham, Eleanor, vii, 62,
  122, 123, 145, 146
Herbarium, 79, 85, 99
Hiberno-English, 66
Higginson, T. W., 2, 4, 85, 113, 121,
  125, 127, 128, 130, 146
high-frequency words, 7
hooks, bell, 107, 108, 114, 117
Howard, William, 3, 62
Hubbard, Melanie, 3, 62
hymn, 29, 30, 70, 71, 72, 73, 74, 89

Index 151

I

immortality, 17, 36, 47, 48, 102, 103, 105, 106, 107, 110, 113, 114, 116, 119, 129, 130, 132, 137, 138
improvisation, 95, 97

J

Jackson, Virginia, 93, 99, 126, 127, 134, 135, 146
jazz, ix, 94, 95, 96, 97
Juhasz, Suzanne, 3, 61, 108, 117, 118

K

Keats, John, x, 20, 93, 119, 123, 127, 128, 129, 130, 131, 132, 133, 134, 135, 136, 139, 141, 143, 144, 146
Keller, Karl, 127, 137, 146
kenning, 14, 15, 17, 51, 52, 54, 58
Knox, Helene Margrethe, 16, 61
Kubrin, Charis E., 112, 113, 118

L

Lathrop, Tad, 99
Leyda, Jay, 76, 77, 99
Lindberg-Seyersted, 3, 62
Loeffelholz, Mary, 93, 99, 134
Lord, 12, 15, 30, 34, 47, 51, 105, 128, 137, 142, 143
Lundin, Roger, 102, 103, 118

M

Matthews, Cerys, 68, 99
McDowell, Marta, 77, 99
McMahon, April M. S., 16, 61
McNaughton, Ruth Flanders, 93, 99

metaphor, 6, 13, 14, 15, 16, 52, 53, 54, 55, 56, 57, 58, 59, 86, 87, 88, 90, 91, 92, 93, 97, 110
metonymy, ix, 16, 17
Miller, Cristanne, 3, 62, 68, 73, 87, 99, 111, 117, 118, 126, 139, 140, 141, 145, 146
Miller, Ruth, 125, 146
Monte, Steven, 3, 62
Mount Holyoke Female Seminary, 13, 69, 75, 102
Murray, Aife, 66, 99
music binder, 80, 94

N

names, 2, 10, 11, 12, 13, 17, 131
nature, x, 1, 8, 9, 10, 11, 13, 18, 29, 49, 66, 70, 74, 76, 77, 80, 82, 86, 89, 90, 92, 93, 97, 102, 103, 110, 119, 121, 127, 128, 129, 131, 134, 136, 139, 141, 143, 144
Newman, Samuel Phillips, 2, 61, 94
noun, 3, 5, 6, 7, 14, 15, 16, 17

O

O'Maley, Carrie, 140, 146
Oberhaus, Dorothy Huff, 122, 147
organ, 86, 89, 92

P

Paglia, Camille, 95, 99
Pareles, Jon, 115, 118
Pellegrinelli, Lara, 96, 97, 99
person name, ix, 3, 10, 11, 12, 13, 14
Petrino, Elizabeth, x, 127, 128, 129, 131, 132, 135, 145, 146
Phillips, Elizabeth, 61, 67, 99

philology, 2, 17, 18, 62
piano, 68, 69, 75, 76, 79, 80, 81, 82, 83, 85, 86, 91, 94, 95, 96
poetic inspiration, x, 119, 126, 134, 140
polyglot, ix, 65, 95

Q

Quinn, Eithne, 96, 105, 118

R

Reglin, Louise Winn, 87, 99
Rich, Adrienne, 91, 100
Rockstro, William S., 90, 100
Romney, Rebecca, 14, 15, 61, 138
Rosenthal, M. L., 124, 147
Ross, Christine, 3, 62
Rossetti, Christina, 6, 61

S

Scheurer, Erika, 2, 62
Scheurich, Neil, 102, 103, 106, 110, 118
Severn, Joseph, 127, 130, 132, 146
Sewall, Richard B., 2, 4, 61, 94, 100, 102, 118
Sharon-Zisser, Shirley, 3, 63
Short, Bryan, 7, 61, 66, 72, 100
Shurr, William, 121, 147
singing, 17, 51, 69, 70, 75, 76, 78, 80, 87, 93
Small, Judy Jo, 3, 63, 78, 100
Socarides, Alexandra, vii, 125, 126, 146

St. Armand, Barton Levi, 88, 100
Steiner, George, 4, 61
Stevenson, Bryan, 107, 118
Swyderski, Ann, 123, 146

T

The Notorious B.I.G., 105, 107, 109, 118
Thoreau, Henry David, 1, 18, 61, 102
Tinajero, Robert, 104, 112, 118
Trench, Richard Chenevix, 1, 63

V

Van Loon, Hendrik Willem, 77, 100
vitality, 2, 3, 10, 13, 116

W

Wardrop, Daneen, 114, 115, 118, 124, 146
Watkins, Calvert, 14, 61
Watts, Isaac, 21, 26, 29, 36, 71, 72, 73, 74, 100
webplay, 5, 6
Webster, Noah, 2, 3, 4, 5, 6, 7, 16, 25, 61, 62, 89, 92, 100, 136, 147
Werning, Marcus, 7, 62
Whicher, George, 77, 100
White, Fred, 66, 100
Whitman, Walt, 1, 62, 102
Willis, Elizabeth, 73, 100
Wohlpart, James A., 123, 147
Wolosky, Shira, 87, 100, 102, 103, 127, 147

www.ingramcontent.com/pod-product-compliance
Lightning Source LLC
Chambersburg PA
CBHW061451300426
44114CB00014B/1930